The Idea of the Good in Platonic-Aristotelian Philosophy

THE
IDEA OF THE GOOD
IN
PLATONIC-ARISTOTELIAN
PHILOSOPHY

HANS-GEORG GADAMER

TRANSLATED AND WITH AN
INTRODUCTION AND ANNOTATION
BY P. CHRISTOPHER SMITH

YALE UNIVERSITY PRESS
NEW HAVEN AND LONDON

The preparation of this volume was made possible
in part by a grant from the Program for
Translations of the National
Endowment for the Humanities,
an independent federal agency.

Originally published in German by J. C. B. Mohr (Paul Siebeck).

Designed by Sally Harris
and set in Sabon type by Eastern Graphics.
Printed in the United States of America by
Vail-Ballou Press, Binghamton, N.Y.

Library of Congress Cataloging-in-Publication Data

Gadamer, Hans Georg, 1900–
The idea of the good in
Platonic-Aristotelian philosophy.
Translation of: Die Idee des Guten
zwischen Plato und Aristoteles.
Includes index.
1. Plato—Contributions in ethics—Addresses, essays,
lectures. 2. Aristotle—Contributions in ethics—
Addresses, essays, lectures. 3. Ethics, Ancient—
Addresses, essays, lectures. I. Title.
B398.E8G2913 1986   170   85–22710
ISBNs 0–300–03463–6 (cloth)
0–300–04114–4 (pbk.)

3 5 7 9 10 8 6 4

CONTENTS

TRANSLATOR'S
INTRODUCTION

Though shorter than *Truth and Method*[1] and, as Gadamer readily acknowledges, not a completely unified study, *The Idea of the Good in Platonic-Aristotelian Philosophy*[2] must be counted nonetheless among Gadamer's most important books. For one thing, it gives us an extended example of the hermeneutical or interpretive techniques for which Gadamer has become so well known; for another, it provides us with remarkable new insights

---

1. Hans Georg Gadamer, *Wahrheit und Methode* (Tübingen, 1965), henceforth *WM*. This work has appeared in translation as *Truth and Method* (New York, 1975). Translations of passages cited here are my own.

2. Gadamer, *Die Idee des Guten zwischen Plato und Aristoteles* (Heidelberg, 1978). The *zwischen* is difficult to render in ordinary English. "Between," naturally, will not do, and Gadamer intentionally avoids the more common "von . . . zu" (from . . . to) and "in." He found the circumlocution I have used here appropriate for two reasons, which should become clearer in the course of this introduction. Briefly, he gives priority not to the individual authors as such, but to the thought we find expressed in their works. Hence he tends to say "the Socratic question" and "Platonic philosophy" rather than Socrates' question and Plato's philosophy. Furthermore, he includes expositions of texts whose authorship may be contested, for example, the *Magna Moralia*, but whose content is clearly Platonic or Aristotelian "heritage." He also wants to stress that one should not approach these thinkers "developmentally," which is to say, in a way that makes it appear that Aristotle broke with Plato. Instead, he contends, it is best to think of a shared, continuous tradition to which both belong. In short, the choice of *zwischen* is meant, above all, to set off Gadamer's approach from that of Werner Jaeger. See Jaeger, *Aristoteles, Grundlegung einer Geschichte seiner Entwicklung* (Berlin, 1923), translated as *Aristotle: Fundamentals of the History of his Development* (London, 1948).

into what Platonic-Aristotelian philosophy was about. But, most significantly, since it is concerned in large part with the relationship between theory and practice and with "the good," it introduces us to the ethical dimension in Gadamer's thinking.

Truth and Method, of course, had a great deal to say about moral philosophy, and particular attention is given there to Aristotle's idea of *phronēsis*, or moral reasonableness. But Gadamer's intent in that book was to point out that interpretation of works of art and historical texts could not proceed according to the method of the natural sciences, and that the truths contained in these works and texts were of a different sort from those discovered in science. In *Truth and Method* he turns to phronēsis primarily because Aristotle shows that it, too, must be distinguished from scientific reasoning insofar as it has its own distinct way of relating to the truth (*alētheuein*). Thus Aristotle's moral understanding serves in *Truth and Method* as an example of the general theory of nonscientific understanding that Gadamer wishes to elaborate. Here, in contrast, phronēsis is investigated for its own sake, and Gadamer turns expressly to the good in human life, the theme of his first book, *Platos dialektische Ethik*:[3] Hence we find in *The Idea of the Good in Platonic-Aristotelian Philosophy* not only a continuation of the things we

---

3. *Platos dialektische Ethik. Phänomenologische Interpretationen zum 'Philebus'*, (Hamburg, 1931) and republished in *Platos dialektische Ethik* (Hamburg, 1968), henceforth *PDE*, pp. xiii–178.

Other works by Gadamer bearing on the subject matter of this book are:

"Zur Vorgeschichte der Metaphysik," in *Um die Bergriffswelt der Vorsokratiker* (Darmstadt, 1968), pp. 364–90.

"Antike Atomtheorie," in ibid., pp. 512–33.

"Plato und die Dichter," in *PDE*, pp. 181–204, translated as "Plato and the Poets," in *Dialogue and Dialectic* (New Haven, 1980), henceforth *DD*, pp. 39–72.

have come to expect in Gadamer's work, his interpretive artistry and his reliance upon, and extraordinary grasp of, Greek thought, but also an investigation of moral philosophy— its premises, its subject matter, and its applications. With regard to the principles of Gadamer's hermeneutics, we find two especially well displayed here. First, particular attention

---

"Platos Staat der Erziehung," in *PDE*, pp. 205–20, translated as "Plato's Educational State," in *DD*, pp. 73–92.

"Dialektik und Sophistik im VII. platonischen Brief," in *PDE*, pp. 221–48, translated as "Dialectic and Sophism in Plato's *Seventh Letter*," in *DD*, pp. 93–123.

"*Amicus Plato Magis Amica Veritas,*" in *PDE*, pp. 249–69, translated with same title in *DD*, pp. 194–218.

"Vorgestalten der Reflexion," in *Kleine Schriften*, 4 vols. (Tübingen, 1967–77) henceforth *KS*, vol. 3, pp. 1–13.

"Platon und die Vorsokratiker," in *KS*, vol. 3, pp. 14–26.

"*Logos* und *Ergon* im platonisichen 'Lysis,'" in *KS*, vol. 3, pp. 50–63, translated as "*Logos* and *Ergon* in Plato's *Lysis*," in *DD*, pp. 1–20.

"Platons ungeschriebene Dialektik," in *KS*, vol. 3, pp. 27–49, translated as "Plato's Unwritten Dialectic," in *DD*, pp. 124–55.

"Über das Göttliche im frühen Denken der Griechen," in *KS*, vol. 3, pp. 64–79.

"Gibt es die Materie? Eine Studie zur Begriffsbildung in Philosophie und Wissenschaft," in *Convivium Cosmologicum* (Basel, 1973), pp. 93–109.

"Die Unsterblichkeitsbeweise in Platons 'Phaidon'," in *Wirklichkeit und Reflexion* (Pfullingen, 1973), pp. 145–61, translated as "The Proofs of Immortality in Plato's *Phaedo*," in *DD*, pp. 21–38.

"Idee und Wirklichkeit in Platos 'Timaios'" in *Sitzungsberichte der Heidelberger Akademie der Wissenschaften* (Heidelberg, 1974), translated as "Idea and Reality in Plato's *Timaeus*," in *DD*, pp. 156–93.

"Vom Anfang bei Heraklit," in *Sein und Geschichtlichkeit* (Frankfurt, 1974), pp. 166–75.

"Philosophie und Religion im griechischen Altertum," in *Festschrift* paper for Wilhelm Anz, 1975, unpublished.

See also numerous references to Plato and Aristotle in *Warheit und Methode* and in *Hegels Dialektik* (Tübingen, 1971), translated as *Hegel's Dialectic* (New Haven, 1976), henceforth *HD*.

is paid in each case to the *kind* of text we are interpreting. That attention is especially called for here, since any attempt to understand what Plato and Aristotle are saying must confront the problem of the disparate nature of the extant texts, the fact that we have fictional dialogues from Plato and a mixture of treatises and lecture notes from Aristotle. Even the differences among the texts from Aristotle must be carefully taken into account. Gadamer points out, for instance, that the *Magna Moralia*, since it is in the form of lecture notes, or perhaps even class notes by someone else, cannot be read with the logical and compositional expectations that one brings to the other ethical treatises, for, as notes, they depend on what Aristotle would have said in his lectures to fill them out. Most important of all textual differences, however, is the distinction between Plato's mythical, metaphorical way of putting things and Aristotle's "cautious" conceptualizations—of natural phenomena, on the one hand, and the phenomena of our practical life, on the other. It is precisely the failure to observe this distinction that has misled us into taking what Plato says in the dialogues as statements and then comparing these to the supposedly equivalent statements made by Aristotle. As Gadamer points out (*WM* 444), anyone who has seen what comes back in recorded "statements"—in a court proceeding, say—will see at once that taking what someone says as a statement is more likely to obscure what he or she was getting at than to display it. *Mis*interpretation will be inevitable.

The most unfortunate consequence of comparing Plato and Aristotle in this way has been that the two thinkers have been put at odds not only with each other, but also with themselves. Both are said to have "developed" beyond, and subsequently taken back, their earlier positions, and this thesis has been supported by contrasting statements from later works with statements from earlier works. As Gadamer sees it, there must be something wrong here. For one thing, before the modern period (Galileo) no one thought of putting the two thinkers in opposition to each other.[4] For another, the ancient tradition reports no such modification of the views of either one of them. Hence it is far more promising, Gadamer argues, to assume that they were consistent, with themselves and with each other, in "getting at" the same thing, albeit in quite different modes of discourse. The task then becomes to find out what that same thing is and to display it as it shows up in Plato's and Aristotle's diverse presentations. Here two influences on Gadamer's thought become evident at once: above all Husserl, of course, but also, I suggest, Rudolf Bultmann. Gadamer will use the "workman-like" techniques of Husserl's phenomenological description to bring to light the common subject matter of Platonic-Aristotelian thought. And in Plato's case that means that he will have to be "demythologized," to use Bultmann's term—that is, what he says metaphorically will have to be translated into conceptualizations of the phenomena of our existence, the kind of conceptualizations that Aristotle was attempting.

But it is not only inattentiveness to textual differences that is responsible for the misunderstanding that pits Plato and Aristotle against each other. The misunderstanding is also the result of failure to establish the occasion for what is said in each case. With that we come to the second hermeneutical principle exemplified in this book. The principal problem with reducing any form of discourse to a series of statements is that the context or setting, which alone gives what is said its meaning, is thereby omitted. Naturally, we face this problem with any written text: in order to know what was said, we need to know what it was

4. The modern period is faced with a new problem: how to overcome teleological science. Galileo is thus led to play off the Pythagorean-mathematical in Plato against Aristotelian physics. See Gadamer, *Dialogue and Dialectic*, p. 195.

said in response to, and, more often than not, written texts do not tell us this expressly. They have come down to us as excerpts, as it were, even if, prima facie, they are complete in themselves. Hence, for someone who would understand them, the task is to put them back in their setting. Said another way, one must give priority to the question being addressed over the answer to it contained in the text; precisely what is unsaid and tacitly presupposed must be brought to the fore. Thus Gadamer replaces propositional logic's testing of statements with "the logic of question and answer" (cf. *WM* 351 ff.).

Gadamer applies this principle of interpretation in several ways. On the other hand, he often takes into account those things which are meant precisely by *not* being said, that is, "indirect" or "negative" meanings, as he calls them. The paradigm here is satire, of which he finds a good deal in Plato's *Republic*; the absurdly impractical proposals that Plato makes there can only be understood as satirical inversions of the perversions of political life in the Athens of that time. That is to say, they can only be understood "e contrario."[5] But, more generally, he finds it imperative to treat anything that Plato or Aristotle says as an answer to a particular question posed. If we are to understand what they are saying, this question must be uncovered and specified.

It turns out that Plato and Aristotle are answering questions posed somewhat differently, and that is the primary reason for

---

5. The phrase "e contrario" epitomizes one important sense of the word "dialectical" in Gadamer: one must read satire "dialectically," which is to say, as the contrary of what is meant. But not only satire. Gadamer's analysis of Hegel's "Verkehrte Welt" (inverted-perverted world) provides a masterful exposition of this principle of dialectical reading (see Gadamer, *Hegel's Dialectic*, pp. 35–53). And Socratic irony, of course, is another prime example of something which must be understood e contrario.

the apparent differences in their thinking. Though Gadamer does not cite the passage explicitly, Aristotle gives us a decisive clue in *Metaphysics*, Alpha 6, where he says that Plato extended Socrates' concern with invariant moral truths to the whole of nature. Gadamer's thesis is that Plato is responding in the whole of what he says to a near-total moral dissolution in his society and to the concurrent sophistic rhetorical techniques that confound any real moral reasoning and substitute for it more or less disguised rationalizations of cupidity and the unbridled will to power. This advent of sophism is the occasion for his thought. Consequently, Plato turned to mathematics, for he saw there a kind of reasoning that was self-evidently invulnerable to sophistic "tricks," and which in its structure must be similar to the unshakable reasoning by means of which Socartes held to what he knew to be right. Aristotle, on the other hand, is responding to theoretical questions, for his thinking is prompted by wonderment (*thaumazein*) not political alienation. Hence he wishes to display the analogical structures of things in a variety of realms, among them the world of nature and, in distinction to that world, the human practical world. The "descriptive caution" appropriate to his task leads him to divorce these realms, to distinguish sharply between the methods and objects of inquiry appropriate to each, and to fault Plato precisely for not making these distinctions, for example, for importing the ontological idea of the good into practical considerations where it has no application.

Thus, if Plato argues theoretically against the Pythagoreans' failure to distinguish between the perceived thing and the noetic "number"—their failure, that is, to separate the pure arithmetical relationship from the imperfect example of it—he does so, in the final analysis, in order to head off confusing sophistic talk and to be able, like Socrates, to hold to what is morally true despite appearances to the contrary that some clever speaker may conjure up. But there is no occasion for Aristotle to make such a separation (*chōrismos*), since he is addressing questions raised by the particular phenomena he is investigating, and here, too, he is consequently critical of Plato. His starting point, unlike Plato's, is the specific "this-whatever" (*tode ti*) and the fact "that . . ." (*hote* . . .). Thus Aristotle's critique of Plato is not so much indicative of serious philosophical differences as of the fact that, given the questions he was raising, he could not find any application of Plato's conclusions, especially those concerning his "separated" idea of the good.

Now if one sorts these things out properly, the result is surprising: in the end there is a "same thing," Gadamer finds, which both Plato and Aristotle are elaborating, despite the different occasions for their doing so and their different ways of doing it— namely, the world as it becomes clear to us in our speaking of it. Plato and Aristotle both belong to the unified tradition of *logos* philosophy. In the *Phaedo* Plato's Socrates turns away from naturalistic accounts of things to the logoi, our ways of speaking; similarly, Aristotle founds his investigations on *"pōs legetai,"* how something is spoken of. Furthermore, both Plato and Aristotle concern themselves with the invariant *eidos*, the form which answers the central question that arises in our speaking of anything, namely, *"ti estin?"* ("what is it?"). To be sure, Plato turns to the mathematical in his initial response to the moral threat of sophism, but it is clear as early as the *Phaedo*, in which Plato's Socrates engages two mathematically oriented Pythagoreans in discussion of the eidē (forms), that the cosmos too is to be understood in terms of our moral experience. When Socrates, in leading up to the hypothesis of the eidos (form), describes his turn to the logoi (96a ff.), he says that he was pursuing an account of nature (*peri physeōs historia*), and that he was attracted to Anaxagoras because the latter, so it seemed, wanted to account for natural things in terms of what is best (*beltiston*) for them (97c). Hence Anaxagoras's *nous* (mind) promised, albeit deceptively, to overcome the deficiencies of merely physiological causal accounts. Aristotle, on the other hand, begins with "what is by nature," the *physei onta*, in responding primarily to theoretical questions. Yet ultimately Aristotle too may be said to have extended Socrates' and Plato's question concerning *aretē* (virtue) and the good or best (*ariston*) in his investigations of the universe: the "physicists" (*physikoi*), he says, with only two kinds of explanation at their disposal— from what, and by the agency of what—could not properly grasp the cosmos, in which things occur for the sake of (*heneka*) what is good.

It remains now to specify briefly how Gadamer arrives at these conclusions. I offer here an overview of Gadamer's argument since it often seems highly compressed and, in any event, is sometimes difficult to follow once one is immersed in the details of it.

In regard to Plato, what is emphasized above all is the continuity of his thought. Gadamer adheres to the traditional chronology assigned to Plato's dialogues but not to the prevailing twentieth-century theory that this chronology can be arrived at by establishing turning points at which Plato is supposed to have distanced himself from positions he had taken previously. On the contrary, he maintains, there is continuity in the line of thought unfolded in Plato's work. What varies is only the way he chooses to get at his subject matter.

To begin with there are the refutational, or elenchtic, dialogues, in which Socrates confronts the great sophists of his time—Protagoras, Gorgias, Callicles, Thrasymachus—and displays the emptiness of their claims to be able to teach virtue. In truth theirs is a technical mentality, and what they teach is only a *technē* (art) of succeeding. The conclusion to be drawn from these dialogues—at times explicit, but more often implied negatively or indirectly—is that knowledge in virtue is somehow different from knowledge in technē. This shows up above all in the fact that virtue cannot be taught. And there is a further truth that emerges here, again largely unsaid, that the traditional ideas of aretē upon which the sophists rely and which might be learned by imitating a paragon have become groundless and susceptible of sophistic dissimulation. Therefore, to withstand seduction by self-interest and by otherwise insatiable desires for sensuous gratification and power, to which sophism panders, one must now be able to give justification for what is good, that is, justification for one's choices of what is right as opposed to what is wrong. But nobody seems to know how to do that, least of all those sophists who claim that they do.

The primary concern in these elenchtic dialogues, then, is a practical one, and that makes the *Phaedo* and the *Republic*, in which the concern seems to shift to epistemological and ontological matters, appear to mark a definite transition in Plato's thought. For in these next works the "ideas" are introduced, and in the *Republic* even the "idea of ideas," the idea of the good, which would seem to serve as a first principle of both true knowledge and true reality. In the twentieth-century traditions of Plato interpretation—particularly the neo-Kantian, which found support for its theory of science in this "stage" of Plato— would have it that the question Plato is addressing here is a new, theoretical one no longer related to the Socratic question concerning aretē. But Gadamer sees a serious oversight here. A careful reading, he argues, shows that Plato is still dealing with the same issue. Gadamer maintains that both the hypthesis of the eidos in the *Phaedo* and the *Republic's* discussion of a training in dialectic leading up to the idea of the good do in fact follow from the concern with aretē. (The problem here is one of long standing, for Aristotle himself argued that Plato's introduction of the question of aretē in his lecture "On the Good" led to an incoherence, which would make it appear that the idea of the good is a purely ontological doctrine that has no connection with the practical question of aretē.)

In regard to the *Republic*, Gadamer points out that the extension of the discussion beyond book 4 does seem to have something arbitrary about it, in that book 4's discussion of the unity of the virtues in knowledge is not continued, nor is what follows tied in to, or derived from, this discussion. The concern is now the theoretical education of the guardians, an education which in book 6 will lead them out of the impure world of practical matters, the shadowy "cave," into the pure world of the forms. Whether intended or not, the discussion here would seem to result in an absolute antithesis of theory and practice. Moreover, there seems no doubt that, as a way of life, the former is far superior to the latter in Plato's eyes.

Gadamer maintains, however, that if one asks what question is actually being addressed in the allegory of the cave, one sees that the concern is not just, or even primarily, a theoretical, scientific one, but in fact an existential-practical question of holding steadfastly to the truth in the face of tests or refutations (*elenchoi*), much as a soldier holds his ground in battle or a wrestler stands firm against attempts to throw him—this is the language Plato uses here. And what are these tests of mettle? The guardians will find themselves in a conflict between honest execution of the duties of their office for the public weal and the "pursuit of power after power," as we in the English-speaking world might put it, using the words of Thomas Hobbes. The guardians, in other words, will be tested by the flattery of both their own desires for gratification and sophistic sycophants, flattery that might seduce them into sacrificing their integrity. It is precisely this flattery that they must be educated to withstand.

In short, it turns out that the theory of dialectic in which they are to be trained is a way of distinguishing and, above all, of distinguishing practically between right and wrong, good and bad. To do that, the guardians must know the idea of the good, for that idea is exactly what those in the cave do not know. The cave-dwellers' technai (arts) give them the knowledge "how to" do something, knowledge of the means to an end, but not knowledge of the end itself, the *hou heneka*, the "what for." And without this knowledge, knowledge of the good, the guardians, like the cave-dwellers, will succumb to the particular urgings of their self-interest. Thus, knowledge of the good turns out to be not just a theoretical insight, not just a matter of logos (reasoning). It is a principle in *ergon* (deed) and makes possible constancy in the choice of the life that one leads (Aristotle: *prohairesis tou biou*).

And now the real meaning of the hypothesis of the eidos in the *Phaedo* becomes evident. As opposed to what the neo-Kantian school might have seen in it, the hypothesis of the eidos is not at all the "scientific" postulation of a universal idea that is to be verified by the facts. As in the *Republic*, the issue in the *Phaedo* is how to head off whatever might mislead us, how to head off sophistic talk, and this can be done only if we know what the eidos of the thing we are speaking of includes and what it excludes, what pertains to it and what does not. Hypothesizing the eidos thus has nothing to do with empirical verification but, instead, with making precisely these eidetic distinctions. The method of hypothesis is thus dialectic, and it allows us to hold undisconcertedly to what is meant, just as dialectic in the *Republic* enabled the guardians to hold undisconcertedly to what is good. The paradigm for steadfastness in both cases remains

Socrates, who was not to be dissuaded from what he saw to be right, no matter what arguments concerning his own "advantage" might be adanced. His aretē was such that he would not even accept the escape from death offered to him by his friends.

In this way it is possible to establish a continuous line leading to the 'later' *Philebus*. It will be noted that this dialogue too begins with an ethical issue—whether the good life is one of pleasure or of intellect or of some third thing—and it also involves its interlocutors in the task of giving justification for their contentions concerning the good life, justification that will make their arguments invulnerable to the sophistic arts of confusing and confounding people with sleights of hand that interchange the one and the many.[6] The way for us to head off such eristic "tricks"—the "Promethean fire," as Socrates calls it—is to know just what number (*arithmos*) of things is included in the "one" thing we are speaking of, and thus what is to be excluded as extraneous. This knowledge correlates precisely with what was said about the hypothesis of the eidos in the *Phaedo*.

Still, the introduction of the *arithmos* clearly leads to ontological considerations that transcend the practical questions that initially occasioned this dialogue. The question about human existence now becomes a question about the structure of the whole cosmos, a structure of which human existence is just one example. Hence the *Philebus* brings into sharper focus the problem that had already surfaced in the *Republic* concerning the relationship between the theoretical-ontological and the practical. The guardians, we learn there, are to be trained in dialectic, which is to say, in the knowledge that comes after they have

6. One should not overlook the fact that the *Sophist*, a later dialogue whose principal concern seemed to some (for example, F. Cornford) to be with ontological questions, in fact focuses on sophistic deception, and that the heady ontological issues it raises continue to be occasioned by the threat of sophism.

passed through training in the theoretical dianoetic sciences and
that would appear to be the culmination of the latter. Put another way, in the *Republic* dialectic and knowledge of the good
are theoretical knowledge about reality, about being, and seem
at first glance far removed from any practical concerns. And in
the *Philebus* too the question again becomes the same one raised
by Aristotle in regard to Plato's "On the Good," namely, what
such purely theoretical matters as the doctrine of number, the
"one" and the "indeterminate two," the *peras* (limit) and the
apeiron (unlimited, indefinite)—all of which appeared in "On
the Good" as well as in the *Philebus*— could possibly have to do
with the Socratic question about aretē.

    An answer will be forthcoming, Gadamer suggests, if one first
makes clear just what these theoretical doctrines mean, but clarity can be obtained only if one translates Plato's myths and metaphors into conceptual language. Here the techniques of Husserl's
descriptive phenomenology can be put to good use, for the task
is to display the phenomenon that Plato is getting at. In the
Philebus Plato speaks of the good as the structure of a "mixture"
someone might brew, the "potion" as it were, which is our human life. The various "ingredients," the kinds of pleasure and intellect, are not to be mixed indiscriminately, but well. That they
are not means that a limit must be set: not an indeterminate
number, but only "so and so many," a specific arithmos, will be
admitted. A "good" mixture is thus one that has limits set to it,
and the good itself is limitedness (measuredness, or *metriotēs*) in
the midst of constantly threatening indeterminacy and limitless-
ness. Hence not only an ontological principle of the cosmos is
applied when nous sets a limits (*peras*) to the indefinite-unlim-
ited (*to apeiron*) but a principle of the right life as well. As
measuredness, the good in the *Philebus*, we now see, is precisely

Aristotle's mean between the extremes, which is to say, an onto-logical principle with very clear practical relevance.

In anticipating Aristotle's criticisms, it should be noted that, as measuredness, the good in Plato must be distinguished, or "sepa-rated" intellectually, from the mixture itself. But if one abstracts from this metaphor, one finds that, as measuredness, the good is what Hegel calls *ein Moment*, namely, an aspect of something which does not exist separately from it. In short, it is *in* the thing of which it is the structure. Thus, when we say that it is *chōriston* (separate), we are not denying that it is in the thing. We are say-ing only that it must be distinguished from the thing in our thinking—something that Aristotle would be the last to deny. For he too raises the question *ti estin* ("what is it?"), a question aimed at distinguishing the invariable *Moment*, the "what" (*ti*) in any "this-whatever" (*tode ti*).

These striking convergences of Plato's thought with Aristotle's leave us puzzled about Aristotle's critique of Plato. Why would he criticize Plato if in fact he and Plato are saying the same thing? The question raised here is twofold: on the one hand, we must ask what the ontological intent of his critique of Plato's idea of the good is; on the other, we need to know the moral-theoretical intent of that critique.

In resolving this twofold question Gadamer finds it best to hold to the hermeneutical technique of displaying the phenom-ena with which Aristotle's three ethical treatises are con-cerned— the *"mens auctoris"* is of so little importance that the issue of whether all three are by Aristotle himself need not even be raised. The task is to repeat in ourselves (*nachvollziehen*) the steps in the arguments, and thereby to bring to light the thing they are about, what they are aiming at, or, as Husserl and Ga-damer following Husserl put it, their *"Intention."* And it can be established right away that whoever their author might be, they are indeed "about" the same thing.

At the core of the argument in all three is the contention that Plato improperly fuses the ontological and the practical in his applications of the idea of the good. Consequently, it is argued that from the start a clear separation must be made between the practical good and the idea of the good in whatever explanatory function it might have in the universe, and that ethics must be restricted to a consideration of the former. Aristotle justifies this restriction by pointing out that the idea of the good is of no use in the various technai, but this argument, far from weighing against Plato, only affirms Plato's contention that the idea of the good is not accessible to technical knowing, and that knowing the good and knowledge in the technai are radically distinct, a conclusion which, to be sure, was not at all the one "intended" by the Aristotelian line of thought here.

Furthermore, despite his aversion to introducing physics and metaphysics in the ethical treatises, Aristotle constantly finds his arguments drawing him in the direction of ontological considerations which by rights he ought to pursue, but he is prevented from pursuing them by the way in which he was put his question. In the first place, he resorts to the category argument, with the idea of showing that, just as there is no one "being" in itself but only a number of ways in which "is" can be said of something, so too there is no idea of the good, separate (*chōriston*) and for itself, but only a number of ways in which the same word "good" is used. As Gadamer points out, putting things this way raises "uncomfortably more" issues than it should. For when he is expressly pursuing questions of ontology, as he is in the *Categories*, Aristotle maintains that the relationship of the other categories, or ways of using "is," to the central category of "substance" must be clarified, and it would follow that, similarly, the senses of "good" would need to be related to a central sense of the word. Like "is," "is good," which is to say, one and the same expression, is not used in many different ways coincidentally. By rights one would have to ask just what it is that all these uses have in common, but, given the "occasion" and "intention" of Aristotle's argument here, such a question cannot arise.

In the second place, in the ethical treatises Aristotle plainly equates the idea of the good in Plato with the one in Plato's doctrine of the ideal numbers, the one and the indeterminate two, or dyad. He then proceeds to argue that just as it is mistaken to turn the principle of number into a number itself, so Plato is mistaken in turning the principle of good things into another good thing. This argument, too, is essentially ontological.

Here, for his moral-philosophic purposes, that is, of showing that the idea of the good is irrelevant to practice, Aristotle takes Plato's mythological way of putting things literally. In Plato it is said that the numbers "strive" for the one, which makes the one look like an entity. But, as Gadamer's exposition of the *Philebus* shows, the one and the two are principles *in* things, which, nevertheless, are to be distinguished from these things in our thinking—something that Aristotle, were he pursuing questions of ontology, would be the last to deny. Thus they are "for themselves," or chōriston, in a sense, but that does not mean at all that they are separate entities alongside other entities.

And whatever the case may be here, the very presence of these arguments in his ethics shows that there, at least, Aristotle never loses sight of the ontological dimension of the question of the good. His very attempt to expel such considerations from ethics shows "negatively" or "indirectly" that they are important to him. Thus the question of just what the *ariston tōn pantōn*, the good or best of and for all things, might be—the universal,[7] on-tological structure of measuredness in Plato—remains present in Aristotle, despite his stated purpose of limiting himself in his eth-ics to consideration of the *ariston tōn praktōn*, that is, what is good or best in practical matters.

Aristotle, of course, is a consummate phenomenologist who wishes above all to avoid running distinct things together. But is it just his "descriptive caution" that leads him to try to keep on-tological and practical theory separate? Gadamer suggests that there is something else fundamental in Aristotle's way of inquir-ing that leads him to put things as he does, namely, his orienta-tion toward life science. Mathematically oriented thinking such as Plato's would indeed lead to inquiry about the idea of the good as an abstract structure of good things, much as one might inquire about the abstract arithmetical structure of what is num-bered or the abstract principles of harmony in what is harmoni-ous. But that is not the orientation of Aristotle's questioning, which gives primacy precisely to the concrete living thing. Con-sequently, the ariston tōn pantōn for him must not be a concep-tual structure but instead a "mover" of other things, a first real-ity that is not *epeikena tēs ousias*, beyond existence as Plato's idea of the good is, but an existent god. With the postulation of this god, Aristotle does indeed carry out Socrates' demand that we understand the universe starting from our moral experience, that is, that we understand it in terms of what is good, and to

7. Gadamer uses the German *allgemein* in both its English senses, "general" and "universal." I have had to rely on intuition, however fallible, in deciding which to use in the translation, and on occasion I have switched back and forth in the same passage where it seemed that Gadamer had both the more ordinary "general" and the more terminological "universal" in mind. One interesting point: the German *allgemein*—literally "common to all"—tends to sustain Aris-totelian analogical thinking: the form, or eidos, is taken to be *to koinon*, or what all particulars have in common.

this extent he too fuses the practical and the theoretical. But for him this fusion does not mean that a discussion of aretē should lead to a discussion of the cosmos, even though the same sort of structures might be constitutive in both. His concern is not with abstract structures but with the "this here."

In the final chapter, "The Idea of Practical Philosophy," Gadamer addresses the broader issues raised by Aristotle's attempt to exclude any considerations of physics or metaphysics from practical philosophy. This exclusion raises questions about the relationship of the special field of theory that we call practical philosophy, that is, ethics and politics, to theory in general, that is, physics, metaphysics, ontology, and cosmology. How does the application of moral theory, as Aristotle understands it, to moral practice differ from the application of scientific theory, say, in technology or medicine? For the latter may certainly be called practices also, and Aristotle even seems to take technē as a model for practice in general. And just what application does moral theory have in the first place? How does it bear on life as it is actually lived? Finally, what is the relationship between the two lives of reason of which Aristotle speaks, the life of practice and the life of theory? What does Aristotle mean when he calls the life of practical reason a second (*deuteron*) best? Does *deuteron* mean "another," or does it mean "inferior"? Or is its meaning somewhere in between?

The first of these questions is introduced directly by Aristotle's critique of Plato's idea of the good, for a good such as Plato speaks of has, in Aristotle's view, precisely no application to life as it is lived. In medicine all things aim at the specific good of health, at *a* good, but an idea of the good in general is of no use here whatsoever. And so it is with all practices. The good, whichever specific good it might be, must be limited to the specific conditions of particular human practices. Here Aristotle sees a fundamental confusion in Plato, in that he fails to distinguish between the use of "good" in ontology and its use in human practice. (As Gadamer pointed out to me during our discussion of this chapter, according to Aristotle we would have to clearly differentiate between "good" snow insofar as it approaches the ontological good of pure whiteness—perfect snow as snow, as what it means to be snow—and "good" snow in practice, snow that is "good" for skiing, for instance. The ontological sense is wholly irrelevant when there is a question of what ought to be done, for example, of whether one ought to go skiing given the snow conditions.)

So the question comes down to this: What role could there be for practical philosophy, if, as it would seem, each of the specialists would be best equipped to say what is good in their respective technical fields? Put another way, how does doing moral philosophy contribute to aretē, excellence in practice?

With that Gadamer has arrived at a crucial issue in his own thinking, which, perhaps more than anything else, is aimed at pointing out the mistake in making modern scientific technical reasoning the paradigm for all reasoning. The relationship of moral theory to practice is not at all the modern relationship of theory to practice in which an objective, neutral theory can be applied generally to particular problems. In distinction to producing something (*technē, poiēsis*), doing the right thing is not simply an application of general rules,[8] and thus there is some-

---

8. Here Gadamer's thinking is diametrically opposed to the current conception of "moral reasoning" in American philosophy, and, of course, to any attempt to found that conception on Platonic-Aristotelian thought. W. Frankena, for instance, writes in his *Ethics* (Englewood Cliffs, 1973, p. 2): "In this [Socrates'] pattern of moral reasoning [in the *Crito*] one determines what one should do in a particular situation by reference to certain general principles or rules, which one takes as premises from which to deduce a particular conclusion by a

thing misleading about Aristotle's constant allusions to the technai, medicine, military strategy, and so forth. In the first place, as Aristotle recognizes, we need an "appropriate principle" (*oikeia archē*) for moral reasoning, which is not to be confused with mathematical deductive reasoning. For in moral reasoning I always find myself in a particular situation, and the task is not to subsume this particular case under a universal rule which I could know apart from the situation I am in, but to define from within my situation what the general rule is of which this situation is an instance. The particular virtues and virtue in general, as finding the "mean between the extremes," are not universal principles that I apply to a situation, but universalizations of what I am doing when I do what is right. Hence it should be noted carefully that, although Aristotle does indeed speak of the "practical syllogism," he in fact uses this syllogistic reasoning only to exemplify the technical choice of the right means to an end. That he knows, despite his (and Plato's) frequent adversions to the technai, that reasoning here is not to be equated with moral reasonableness is clearly established by his sharp separation of phronēsis from *deinotēs* (*Nicomachean Ethics* 1124a23 ff.). The latter, cleverness, deals with means to an end, and for just that reason, he says, it is to be distinguished from the former, moral reasoning. (In essence, Gadamer finds, Kant makes precisely the same point in distinguishing moral from technical imperatives.)

But how would this generalization of what I am doing when I do what is right contribute to my *doing* what is right? How is this awareness useful? How would it strengthen aretē? The an-

---

kind of practical syllogism, as Aristotle called it. One takes general principles and applies them to individual situations." From Gadamer's point of view, he is completely mistaken.

swer, Gadamer suggests, is to be found in Aristotle's illustration of the archer who is able to hit the mark better precisely because he has chosen a more clearly defined spot on the target at which to aim. When we have learned to fix our sights on precisely what we are doing when we choose what is good, namely, hitting the mean between the extremes, we will choose better. Hence, although moral philosophy enchances ethical training, it is no substitute for it. Just as one must know how to handle a bow and arrow before one can improve one's aim, one must already be behaving morally before moral philosophy will be of any use.

And finally, what is the relationship between the two ideal lives, that of *theōria* and that of *praxis*. Both Plato and Aristotle leave no doubt that the highest, most divine life—the life that for a god would be *teleon* (complete), *hikanon* (sufficient), and thus *haireton* (to be desired or chosen) (*Philebus* 20d)—would be the life of pure theōria. And if one takes that life as the standard against which all else is to be measured, as Plato and Aristotle clearly do, then the life of practice does indeed seem a second best: less complete, insufficient, hence less desirable.

But one must be careful here. As both the *Philebus* and Aristotle's ethical treatises make clear, human beings are not gods, and thus the life that is best for them has to be a life that combines theōria and praxis. Plato portrays human life metaphorically as a "mixture" of reason and pleasure, an image that Aristotle conceptualizes when he speaks of human nature as *syntheton* (composite) (*Nicomachean Ethics* 1177b29). The point that both wish to make—which is the fundamental point of agreement between them concerning the good—is that, in distinction to gods, human beings are always under way toward the divine, or, as Gadamer puts it, their best life is *philosophia*, not *sophia*, that is, striving for wisdom, not wisdom itself. Human beings are finite, not absolute—never absolved from the "remnant of earth" (Goethe) in them that inevitably involves them in the task of living well here in the practical world. Seen this way, the life of praxis is a second best not in the negative sense, but in the sense of one of two "best-nesses" that together constitute the good human life, the life of reason in its combined theoretical and practical functions.

Thus, in both Plato and Aristotle, the good emerges as that toward which we are striving, that for the sake of which (*hou heneka*), that at which we aim (*to telos*). But not only *we*. The whole universe is to be understood as striving for perfection. Thus, in the end, despite his announced separation of practical and physical-metaphysical theory, Aristotle, like Plato, conforms to Socrates' requirement that the universe be understood in terms of our own moral experience, and he too fuses moral theory and ontology: the universe, and not only human experience, is to be thought of in relationship to the good. This cosmic-human good is represented in Plato only quasi-conceptually in his doctrine of the ideal numbers. Aristotle, physikos that he remains and not Pythagorean mathematician, sees the good actualized in the self-mediation of the physei onta with their eidē, the things of nature with their forms. Plato, he argues, separates these forms, and with them the good itself, from the things in which they are realized. This separation, as we will learn here, is a necessity for one who would think mathematically, as Plato does. But indisputably it creates problems (*aporiai*), problems of how the ideas are to be mediated with the appearances, for which Plato provides only metaphorical solutions. Aristotle begins the translation of these metaphors into the context of the investigation of natural things and into the language of concepts.

One should keep in mind that the text of *The Idea of the Good*, as it first appeared in German, was essentially an expanded version of a presentation for a quite select audience (*Die*

Heidelberger Akademie der Wissenschafaten). Its "occasion," in other words, was very different from the "occasion" for the publication of this translation, which, it is hoped, will reach a wide range of English-speaking readers with a variety of interests. I have sought to augment the text both in this introduction and in a number of notes, for often things are omitted which could be expected to be self-evident to its original, narrower audience but are not so for us.

The material for these notes derives in part from my long years of apprenticeship with Professor Gadamer and in part from detailed discussions we had concerning different passages in the text.[9] These discussions provided me with vivid confirmation of Gadamer's thesis, that any written word, like lines in the script of a play, is somehow only dead ink on the page that need to be brought to life by saying it aloud in dialogue. Passages that at first were obscure came to life and became clear in what he had to say about them. I have recorded what I could of these discussions here, but as records, they too are petrified speech, and the train of thought they were meant to elucidate will, I am afraid, sometimes break down. Gadamer has provided me with a number of elaborations of the text that he wished to have inserted in the translation; translations of these are preceded by and conclude with an asterisk. He also made occasional changes in the wording of the original text which I have noted when they are significant. It should be noted too that for the sake of clarity, readability, and style the translation could not be word for word in a number of cases.

A word of caution is in order here, though. It would be inappropriate to expect one continuous, systematically conclusive

9. I am very much indebted to the Translations Division of the National Endowment for the Humanities for making these discussions with Professor Gadamer possible, and indeed this entire project.

line of argument here. For philosophy as Gadamer understands it does not proceed *more geometrico*, as our modern logic, it seems, expects it to.[10] We cannot ascertain an indubitably secured starting point; we cannot know ahead of time where a philosophical discussion will lead us, and we will never be able to say that we have arrived at a definitive conclusion. The starting point is always an open question that is never closed completely. Thus we approach it first with one line of inquiry, then another, all the while aiming to shed light on it from a variety of perspectives, but fully acknowledging that the insights gained in this way will of necessity be inconclusive and unsystematic. Gadamer is serious when he distinguishes the human enterprise of philosophia from divine sophia, and this book is representative of the sensitivity to human finitude and the inevitable discursivity of human thought that leads him, just as it did Plato and Aristotle, to insist on this distinction.

10. As Gadamer pointed out to me, C. Perleman's *The New Rhetoric* (South Bend, 1981) argues convincingly that the Cartesian methodological model, which provides the foundation for much contemporary logic and analytical philosophy in the English-speaking world, in fact falsifies language and discursive reasoning as we actually experience it. S. Toulmin's *An Introduction to Reasoning* (2nd ed., Englewood Cliffs, 1984) represents a major advance in emancipation from Cartesianism insofar as it acknowledges the contextuality of reasoning, that is, the differences in the occasions for it, and recognizes its dialogical, openended character. Even so, he has not quite succeeded in establishing "the hermeneutical priority of the question" (*WM* 344) over the answer-proposition, or "claim" as he calls it. All in all, it appears that, paradoxically, modern physics has long since transcended the Cartesian method, whereas the human sciences and logic, for which it was least appropriate to begin with, remain mired in it. F. A. Heyek makes this point well in regard to economics in his *Studies in Philosophy, Politics, and Economics* (Chicago, 1967).

PREFACE

Hegel, it cannot be denied, did indeed grasp the speculative tendency in both Plato's doctrine of the ideas and Aristotle's substance ontology, since his thinking was so congenial to theirs. And to that extent he is the first in modern times to break through the schema of interpretation of Plato's doctrine of the ideas shaped by Aristotle and further developed in Neoplatonism and the Christian tradition. Nor can one say that Hegel has remained without any lasting influence on scholarship in the history of philosophy. Such good Aristotelians as Trendelenburg and Eduard Zeller owe him a great deal. Above all, Hegel was the first to make the philosophical significance of Plato's "esoteric," "dialectical" dialogues accessible. However, the unitary effect[1] connecting Plato's and Aristotle's logos philosophy—

---

1. *Wirkungseinheit.* The word is related to Gadamer's concept *Wirkungsgeschichte,* the history of effects. The point is that far from being opposed to each other, Plato and Aristotle belong to a continuous line of thought. They have in mind the same subject matter, or *Sache.* Hence, rather than stressing the individual contributions of each, Gadamer finds it best to ask just what that subject matter is which concerns both thinkers, and to explicate it phenomenologically. One further point regarding *Wirkung,* or effect: since it is the subject matter and not the indidivudal thinker that is primary, one must be careful to read "effect" not as the effect that a thinker has on subsequent thinkers, but as the effect that the subject matter, as it is passed on by tradition, has on an individual. It is not the thinking subject that comes first, but the tradition that makes his or her thought possible. Accordingly, Gadamer's *wirkungsgeschichtliches Bewusstsein* might best be translated not as "historically effec*tive,*" but as "historically ef*fected* consciousness." TRANSLATOR.

1

which did not remain hidden from Hegel—was underestimated, it seems to me, in the period following him and continues to be until this day.

There are various reasons why. To be sure, there was a concealed, unacknowledged Hegelianism behind the neo-Kantian interpretations of Plato in Cohen and Natorp and in their successors Cassirer, N. Hartmann, Hönigswald, and Stenzel. But given their particular mentality, it was exclusively Plato, and not in the least Aristotle, who could sustain this generation of scholars, in their critical-idealistic purposes. A complete elaboration of Hegel's insights was totally obstructed, on the one hand, by the dogmatic overlay superimposed on Aristotle by the neo-Thomism prevailing in the Catholic camp, and on the other, by the hereditary feud between modern natural science and the Aristotelian teleological understanding of nature or, in fact, any idealistic philosophy of nature. Furthermore, when it interpreted the "idea" as the "natural law," thereby bringing together Plato and Galileo, the neo-Kantian interpretation of Plato, especially that of Natorp, proceeded all too provocatively with the Greek text while remaining insensitive to historical differences. If one starts from this idealistic neo-Kantian interpretation of Plato, then Aristotle's critique of Plato can appear only as an absurd misunderstanding. This fact further contributed to the failure to recognize the unitary effect in Plato and Aristotle, thereby blocking a full incorporation of the Greek heritage into our own philosophical thought. Such trivial and naive juxtapositions as "Plato, the idealist," versus "Aristotle, the realist," gained universal currency, although they actually only confirmed the truly abysmal depth of prejudice in any idealism of consciousness.[2] In addition,

---

2. The goal of neo-Kantianism was to develop the "transcendental" forms that consciousness applies in constituting its objects. Neo-Kantians seized upon

the schema for which Hegel provided the inspiration which construed Greek thought as not yet able to conceive of the absolute
as spirit, life, and self-consciousness, did not promote a proper
evaluation of the fundamental significance of Greek thought for
modern philosophy.

Nicolai Hartmann's dissociation of himself from neo-Kantian
idealism stimulated me to try to penetrate Aristotle's thought,
and the French and English research—of Robin, Taylor, Ross,
Hardie, and, above all, the incomparable Hicks—proved most
helpful in my endeavors. At that time, however, I fell far short of
seeing the unity in the logos philosophy, which started with
Socrates' questioning and then quickly deteriorated in the post-
Aristotelian period, but which, nevertheless, permanently determined the entire conceptual apparatus of Western thought. En-
countering Heidegger turned out to be decisive for me at that
stage. Heidegger had worked his way through both the Catholic-

---

Plato's idealism precisely because it appeared to them that Plato had set out to
uncover these same forms of consciousness. Plato's "ideas" were thus understood epistemologically rather than ontically, that is, as transcendental forms of
thought rather than the forms of things in themselves. Aristotle's insistence that
the forms inhere in the things—his doctrine of the *enhylon eidos*—and on the
primacy of the *tode ti* thus seemed to them a regression to a naive realism. When
Gadamer refers to Neo-Kantianism as a mere "idealism of consciousness," he is
implicitly contrasting it with Fichte's and Hegel's idealism, which goes beyond
any epistemic-ontic dichotomy, and which, like Aristotle, whom Hegel favors (cf.
Logik II, "The Logic of the Concept"), views the forms of thought at one and the
same time as the forms of what is, that is, being. Heidegger's break with transcendental philosophy, be it either neo-Kantian or Husserlian, exposed the one-
sidedness of any idealism that founds itself exclusively on our consciousness of
reality. The question to be asked is not how consciousness construes reality, but
how reality, being, presents itself in our awareness of it. The key here is language,
in which that which *is* assumes its form for us. Language is the medium (Gadamer: *Mitte*) in which consciousness and world are joined. Hence it, not consciousness, is the "condition of the possibility" (Kant) of anything's being what it
is. TRANSLATOR.

Aristotelian and neo-Kantian traditions, and in appropriating
Husserl's minutely detailed art of conceptualization, he had
steeled the endurance and power of intuition, which are indispensable for doing philosophy with Aristotle. Here, then, was an
advocate of Aristotle who, in his directness and the freshness of
his phenomenological insights, far surpassed all the traditional
shadings of Aristotelianism, who surpassed Thomism and, yes,
even Hegelianism. To this day hardly anything has been made
public of this event, but it has had its effect on academic teaching, and my own path was defined beginning there. By the time
I published my first book in 1931 [*Platos dialektische Ethik*],
the convergence, at least in the area of practical philosophy, of the
aim of Plato's thinking[3] with Aristotle's conceptual distinctions
had become evident to me.

Even at that time one thing already directed me beyond the
narrower context of problems in practical philosophy, namely,
the methodological problem that our tradition has preserved
two such disparate things as Plato's dialogical compositions and
Aristotle's working drafts. Since we possess neither an authentic
theoretical elaboration of Plato's teachings nor any of the writings that Aristotle published, we must constantly play off two
dissimilar things against each other. The art of phenomenological description, a little of which I was able to learn from Husserl
and Heidegger, helped me in my first attempts to master this

---

3. Plato's *Denkintention*. There is no single felicitous translation here. A
range of things are meant: what Plato and Aristotle had in mind, what their
thought was aiming at, their intent or purpose, and so forth. Denkintention is related to the equally difficult *Sache des Denkens*, or subject matter of thought, the
thing under consideration. The point is that Plato and Aristotle had corrobora-
tive insights into the same truth, though they chose different ways to articulate
and communicate those insights. Hence our task is to get past the differences in
their forms of presentation and to get at what they were both after, so to speak.
TRANSLATOR.

methodological difficulty. Neither *a textual analysis of* the dialogues' mimetic form of communication nor of the protocol
form of Aristotle's papers can chain the authenticity of a descriptive phenomenological exposition based on the text—*a phenomenological exposition of their subject matter itself.*

In the meantime almost half a century has gone by. In many
respects the edge has been taken off the methodological problem—on the Aristotelian side by Werner Jaeger and his school,
and more recently, on the Platonic side by the Tübingen scholars, who received their impetus above all from Robin. The philosophical stimuli I received from Heidegger led me more and
more into the realm of dialectic, Plato's as well as Hegel's. Decades of teaching were devoted to elaborating and testing what I
have called here the Platonic-Aristotelian unitary effect. But in
the background was the continuous challenge posed for me by
the path Heidegger's own thought took, and especially by his interpretation of Plato as the decisive step toward "metaphysical
thought's" obliviousness to being (*Sein*). My elaboration and
projection of a philosophical hermeneutics in *Wahrheit und
Methode* bear witness to my efforts to withstand this challenge
theoretically. The following studies too, it is hoped, will serve to
keep alive both Platonic dialogue and the speculative dimension
common to Plato, Aristotle, and Hegel, as partners in the ongoing discussion which is philosophy. They belong together with a
number of other small building blocks I have gathered in the
meantime.[4]

I have lectured from these studies twice in meetings of the
Heidelberg Academy of Sciences (in 1974 and 1976). What I offer here is a further elaboration of my presentations, to which I
hope to add still other studies. It is unlikely that these will ever

4. See the list of works in n. 3 of the Translator's Introduction.

turn out to be a truly unified work, just as the essay which I offer
here did not, but is instead a series of reflections and observations on the question posed.

It will be noticed that I have referred to recent scholarship
only sparingly. For one thing, I do not feel qualified to take a
comprehensive stand on it. For another, the presuppositions of
my own interpretation are all too different from those of other
research. I ask that the reader take what follows as an attempt to
read the classic Greek thinkers the other way round as it were—
that is, not from the perspective of the assumed superiority of
modernity, which believes itself beyond the ancient philosophers
because it possesses an infinitely refined logic, but instead with
the conviction that philosophy is a human experience that remains the same and that characterizes the human being as such,
and that there is no progress in it, but only participation. That
these things still hold, even for a civilization like ours that is
molded by science, sounds hard to believe, but to me it seems
true nonetheless.

I

THE QUESTION AT ISSUE

If one surveys the last fifty years of research on ancient philosophy—and it has been more than fifty years since Werner Jaeger's book on Aristotle gave new and significant impulses to scholarship in this field—one finds oneself more and more embarrassed by the results of that scholarship. In Werner Jaeger a simple schema still prevailed which gave us the outlines of Aristotle's development from Platonist to critic of Plato's doctrine of the ideas and, finally, to empiricist. Even at that time, to be sure, one could have doubted that this construction was universally valid. But, starting from a literary-historical interpretation of Aristotle's *Metaphysics*, Jaeger extrapolated a line of development backwards and forwards in Aristotle's divergence from the doctrine of the ideas, and it could be said in his favor that his construction was at least unequivocal, not to mention the fact that his analyses exposed the artificiality in the editing of the Aristotelian corpus up to that time. Even then, of course, it was noted that Jaeger's construction yielded a "proto-physics" with far less tangible contours than his "proto-metaphysics," and that the proto-physics was, if seen from the perspective of literary history, not supported convincingly, given the state in which the *Physics* books have come down to us. But most of all [his claim to have found] a "development" in Aristotle's ethics—which Jaeger, with a certain drastic superficiality, managed to fit into his construction by availing himself of only parts of the *Eudem-*

ian Ethics—soon met with well-founded objections. For Jaeger's placement of the *Protrepticus* in this context seemed especially problematical. In the meantime we have J. Düring to compare with.[1] Today it is an established fact that in the entire traditional Aristotelian works we never get back to a point where Aristotle was not a critic of Plato's doctrine of the ideas, but also that we never arrive at a point where he really ceased to be a Platonist. If we start with that fact, then just what it meant to be a "Platonist" once again becomes questionable.

It is inevitable that this difficulty with Aristotle would have a reciprocal effect on our understanding of Plato. Now that our confidence that we can discern developmental phases in Aristotle has pretty well vanished, the question forces itself upon us whether the same thing does not hold for Plato. Is there sufficient foundation for the prevailing historical-genetic way of viewing Plato's writings? These days the dominant view assumes that the dogmatic doctrine of the ideas—which Plato was supposed to have taught at the beginning, and which, with Neoplatonic hues, has shaped our understanding of Platonic philosophy as a theory of two worlds—was later taken back, or at the very least diluted, by Plato himself in his own self-criticism and revision of his teachings. Even today many scholars cling to the belief that Plato's *Parmenides* bears witness to such self-criticism.

It is more or less fatal for this theory, however, that the ancient tradition never reports such a change in views in either Plato or Aristotle—aside from a single observation in the *Metaphysics*, Mu 4, 1078b10 which makes the number theory appear to be a late form of the doctrine of the ideas. Aristotle cites the *Phaedo* just as readily as he does the *Parmenides* or the *Timaeus*

---

1. J. Düring, *Aristotle's Protrepticus. An Attempt at Reconstruction* (Göteborg, 1961).

and seems not to have noticed at all that Plato himself had ever placed his dogmatic theory of the ideas in question. In truth it is almost absurdly obtrusive to the modern reader that the late Plato of the *Parmenides* seems every bit the equal of Aristotle in criticizing the doctrine of the ideas. Even the famous "third man" argument is, as is well known, not only found in the critique of the ideas in Aristotle's *Metaphysics*, but in the *Parmenides* as well. Certainly the worst of all hypotheses is to assume that Aristotle ignored Plato's self-criticism and cold-bloodedly repeated Plato's critical arguments in his own critique of Plato.

The picture looks even worse with regard to the "development" in Aristotle's ethics. Aristotle's presumed evolution from a "politics of the ideas" (in the *Protrepticus*) through a still hesitant distancing of himself from Plato in the *Eudemian Ethics* to the "mature" and self-confident position of the *Nicomachean Ethics* is an arbitrary and contradictory construction of Jaeger's. It is particularly unconvincing if one also brings Plato's late dialogues to bear on the issue, for the *Philebus* and the dialogue on the statesman would be so far in advance of the supposedly Platonizing beginnings of Aristotle's ethics that one can properly ask onself just who is criticizing whom here. The development schema—the postulation of the ideas apart by themselves, then participation of the appearances in the ideas, then dialectic of idea and appearance, and then, at the end, the equating of idea and number—slowly begins to come apart.

Did Plato at first really underestimate the problem in the participation of the appearances in the ideas? Did he teach that the ideas were apart for themselves until one day he recognized that the problem of participation entailed in the postulation of such ideas for themselves was altogether insoluble? Or do both postulations belong together: the ideas being for themselves, the so-called *chōrismos* (separation), and the difficulty, to which one is thereby exposed, concerning participation, or *methexis*, as it is

called? Could it be that chōrismos and methexis go together even
from the start? At the end, in his so-called self-critique, does
Plato not have precisely these two aspects of the subject matter
in mind? And in the *Parmenides* is it not precisely his intent to
fend off the oversimplifications in any dogmatic conception of a
doctrine of the ideas that would like to spare itself the trouble of
dialectic?[2] Might it have been Plato's actual intent in the *Parmenides* to make us so acutely conscious of the ontological problem
in the relationship between idea and appearance that the very in-
appropriateness of the solutions discussed demonstrates the dog-
matism implied in the question itself? In any case, it is striking
that throughout the dialogues the terminology used for the relationship between idea and appearance is extremely free: *parousia* (presence), *symplokē* (interweaving), *koinōnia* (coupling),
methexis (participation), *mimēsis* (imitation), and *mixis* (mixture) are all found alongside each other. Both the *Parmenides*
and Aristotle's critique finally single out *methexis* from these expressions. Plato coins this new word, so it seems, for the "participation" of the particular in the universal, and the problems it
entails are unfolded in the *Parmenides* in particular. Moreover,
that [it was Plato's own word] can virtually be deduced from
Aristotle's observation that Plato followed Pythagorean philosophy, save that where the Pythagoreans spoke of the *mimēsis* of
the things in relationship to numbers—that is, of the visible ex-
emplification of pure numerical relationships in the order of the
heavens and in the theory of musical harmony—Plato, he says,
merely uses another word, namely, *methexis*.[3]

2. The critique of the all too youthful Socrates at *Parmenides* 135d may have
been aimed at making just this point.
3. That the word as such existed in the Ionic form, *metochē*, which Aristotle
uses, is proved by the appearance of it in Herodotus 1. 144. But our concern here
is with its conceptual application.

With this new word, it seems to me, Plato wants to bring out the logical connection of the many to the one, the thing "in common," a connection that was not implied in mimēsis and in the Pythagorean relationship of number and being conceived of as the "approximation [of number] to being" (J. Klein).[4] And beyond that: if we pay attention to Plato's set of synonyms as such, we will have to take *methexis* as well as *mimēsis* more "objectively," *that is, not as "acts" of subjectivity, our ways of conceiving of things, but as real relationships*. *Mimēsis* refers to the existence of what is imitated or represented, while *methexis* refers to coexistence with something. Of course, like the Latin *participatio* and the German *Teilhabe*, the word *methexis* evokes the image of parts. That it does is shown by the early usage of *metechein*.[5] That the part belongs to the whole is precisely what the new word underscores. Even in what is perhaps the earliest allusion to the ideas, in the *Euthyphro*, the question is formulated in such a way that *to hosion* (what is pious), for instance, could be a *morion* (part) of *to dikaion* (what is just).[6] In the first place that means that where one of them is, the other is too: the part is present "in the whole." However Plato is obviously fully aware of the paradox in a participation or taking part (*Teilhabe*) that does not take *a* part, but participates in the whole—as the day participates in the light of the sun. That he is, is shown by the use of that very image in the *Parmenides* and is indirectly confirmed by the set of synonyms I listed above. Indeed, as I

4. J. Klein, "Die griechische Logistik," in *Quellen und Studien zur Geschichte der Mathematik*, vol. 3, no. 1 (1934), and vol. 3, no. 2 (1936).

5. The predominant meaning is plainly to take part in something. But taking part in something along with other things, links all the participants to each other.

6. *Metochē* obviously became terminological later in the academy and precisely in such usage as this where one speaks of the participation of a species in a genus.

have shown elsewhere,[7] the aporia (impenetrable problem) of the whole and the parts always lurks behind the dialectic of idea and appearance, unity and multiplicity.

Aristotle's account, however, implies something else, which he conceals. The change from mimēsis to methexis is not the harmless terminological variation it sounds like it is in Aristotle. On the contrary, it actually reflects the decisive turn which Plato takes: his distinguishing between *aisthēsis* (perception) and *noēsis* (intellection). That is to say, it reflects the step toward mathematics' first comprehension of itself as an "eidetic" science. As long as such a self-understanding had not been achieved—and the Pythagoreans had evidently not achieved it—the numbers could actually appear to be the existing paradigms that the appearances strove to approximate. The "torturing" of strings (*Republic* 531b) expresses this striving quite aptly, but the idea of approximation has something ridiculous about it if one thinks of the 'pure' relationships as such. To say that these are *chōriston* (separate) is to say nothing else than that pure relationships do exist; there is precisely no such thing as a ratio of more or less 1:2.

But if so, mimēsis becomes an inappropriate expression. To be sure, it continues to make sense in a certain metaphorical way if one describes the world of appearances as a mimēsis of pure mathematical relationships, that is, as mere approximations. Thus it remains possible for Plato to use the expression *mimēsis*, together with the pair of concepts copy and paradigm, from the *Phaedo* until the *Timaeus*. *Methexis*, on the other hand, describes things starting from the other side, the being of the pure relationships, and in so doing, it leaves the ontological status of

7. Compare my "Zur Vorgeschichte der Metaphysik," in *Um die Begriffswelt der Vorsokratiker*, pp. 364–90.

what participates undefined. In the *Philebus* it is even possible
for Plato to formulate the ontological status of what participates
as *genesis eis ousian* (coming into being) (26d). Moreover, the
new expression methexis fits better in the context of the long-
standing Eleatic problem of the one, the whole, and being, which
Plato continues to explicate on his own. Therefore Plato accepts
as part of the bargain that the dialectic of the whole and its parts
will inevitably color the relationship of multiplicity and unity:
parts, like members (*ta melē te kai hama merē*) (14e), belong to
the whole whose parts and members they are. That may not say
a great deal, but [even so, we must ask] what bearing it has on
the relationship of the many to the one, that is, on the participation in the idea. The *Philebus* raises this question, and whatever
its solution is supposed to be, a dogmatically rigid conception of
the chōrismos is ruled out by the fact that "the many," which are
not being but *genesis* (becoming), belong to being as parts and
members. This fact does not keep the *holon-meros* (whole-part)
dialectic in Plato from playing a large role elsewhere—in the
Sophist and the *Parmenides* besides the *Philebus*. Using this dialectic, Plato is able to lay bare the multiplicity in the logos of being [the statement of what a thing "is"].[8] As a matter of fact,
even in Parmenides' didactic poem, the whole issue of the logos,
the theme of the "multiplicity" of words (names) for the one Being, is completely obscured. And only Plato's *Sophist* casts light

8. The *logos ousias*, or saying of what a thing is in substance, is examined by
Aristotle in the *Categories*. The significant point for Gadamer is that being is to
be understood starting from the ways in which we speak of something, the ways
something may be *said* to be (Aristotle: *pōs legetai*). Ontology thus becomes inseparable from the philosophical investigation of language. Plato takes the crucial turn here in the *Phaedo*, when his Socrates abandons all naturalistic accounts
of reality and "flees" to the logoi, to our ways of saying things. In what follows,
Gadamer will have much to say about this turn to the logoi, which is at the core
of the "unitary effect" of Platonic-Aristotelian philosophy. TRANSLATOR.

into the darkness here, one step's worth at least, by criticizing
Parmenides and demonstrating the interweaving of the highest
genera.[9]

From what we can extract from the ancient reports about
Plato's students, the same liberality in interpreting the relationship between idea and appearance seems to have prevailed in
Plato's school.[10] We know from Alexander[11] that Euduxus, for
instance, explicitly taught that the ideas were immanent in appearances, and that to make this point he used the concept of
mixis (mixture), which, as a matter of fact, we often find in
Plato's dialogues too. Could it be that Plato's liberality ultimately extended so far that he not only let different theories
stand about the relationship of the ideas to the numbers and to
things but even accepted Aristotle's disputing of the independent
being of the ideas as well? For it is certain surely, and not seriously doubted by anyone today, that from early on Aristotle was
critical of Plato's doctrine of the ideas but nonetheless was, and
remained, a Platonist into his late works.

If one compares Aristotle with the teachings of earlier or later
Greek thinkers, one cannot doubt that all in all he must be
counted as part of the eidos (form) philosophy that Plato established by introducing the ideas and dialectic. Aristotle himself
leaves no doubt in the matter: in his critical overview in *Metaphysics*, Alpha, he finds that the Pythagoreans and Plato were
the first to go beyond the explanatory schema of the

9. For specifics here, see my "Zur Vorgeschichte de Metaphysik."
10. H. J. Krämer has attempted to reconstruct the discussion of this problem
by means of a developmental history in his "Aristoteles und die akademische
Eidoslehre. Zur Geschichte der Universalienprobleme im Platonismus," in *Ar-
chiv für die Geschichte der Philosophie* 55 (1973). (See n. 13 below.)
11. Compare Düring, *Aristotle's Protrepticus*, pp. 244 (with bibliography)
and 253.

"physikoi"—*hylē* (matter) and *hothen hē kinēsis* (whence motion comes)—and he grants Plato and the Pythagoreans their
concept of the *ti estin* (what something is). (For the Pythagoreans, see 987a20, and for Plato, 988a10 and, above all, 988a35.)
Unlike Aristotle, neither the atomists nor Anaxagoras nor the
Stoic school, and perhaps not even a *mathematically oriented*
man like Strato in the Peripatetic school, can be understood
starting with the *legomena* (things we say). In other words, unlike Aristotle, they cannot be interpreted as successors of Plato's
"flight into the *logoi* (ways of saying things)." In opposition to
the privileged ontological status that Plato accords the idea,
Aristotle emphatically asserts that the primary reality is the particular individual, the tode ti (this-something), but even so he remains within the framework of Plato's orientation toward the
logoi. His "primary" substance in no way excludes the eidos.[12]
On the contrary, there is an obvious and indissoluble connection
between that "secondary" substance—the eidos that answers
the question ti estin—and the primary substance of any given
"this."[13]

12. In *"Amicus Plato, Magis Amica Veritas,"* Gadamer argues similarly that
what separates Plato from Aristotle is not at all Plato's emphasis on the eidos and
the idea, for Aristotle emphasizes these no less than Plato. The difference (aside
from their divergent means of presentation) is that Plato approaches the eidos
through mathematics, Aristotle, in contrast, through life science. For Plato the
eidos, as an answer to *ti estin* ("what is it?"), is to be understood in distinction
from its appearances—as mathematical circularity, for example, is to be understood in distinction from circular things. Aristotle, on the other hand, sees the
eidos as that which a living thing (*tode ti*) actualizes as it grows from lack (*sterēsis*) to fulfillment. Thus, for Aristotle, the eidos is one predicate—albeit the
principal one—among many others that may be said of some thing. And as such,
it, unlike circularity, cannot be thought of in separation from the subject of
which it is predicated. TRANSLATOR.
13. It seems risky to me to build an interpretation as extensively upon the
shifting meanings of "primary being" in the *Categories* and the late books of the

Though I am using the concepts of the (disputed) *Categories* for my explication here, I am relying in essence not only on these, but just as much on the central books of the *Metaphysics*, particularly Zeta 6. It is evident too that in Aristotle's eyes there is no contradiction here with his critical demarcation of his own thought from Plato's. The common problem, basic to both Aristotle's and Plato's investigations, is how the logos ousias (the statement of being, of what a thing is) is possible. For my part I would assert that the locution *chōrismos* was never intended to call into question the fact that what is encountered in appearances is always to be thought of in reference to what is invariant in it. The complete separation of a world of the ideas from the world of appearances would be a crass absurdity. If Parmenides, in the dialogue of the same name, consciously pushes us in the direction of that complete separation, he does so, it seems to me, precisely in order to reduce such an understanding of the chōrismos to absurdity (see *Parmenides* 133b ff).

But what, then, is Aristotle's stereotypical objection that Plato hypostasized the universal, his "chōrismos" objection, supposed to mean? Does it really apply to Plato? Just what is the being-for-themselves of the ideas supposed to express in Plato? Does it really imply the opening up of a second world, supposedly separated from our world of appearances by an ontological hiatus? Whatever the answer, things certainly do not stand as the caricature in the *Parmenides* suggests, namely, that this other world of ideas that always are exists only for gods who always are, and our sensory world of fleeting appearances only for mortal human beings. That the ideas are ideas *of* appearances and that they do not constitute a world existing for itself are expressed

---

Metaphysics as H. J. Krämer has done in his admirable and perceptive essay "Aristoteles und die akademische Eidoslehre."

negatively by Plato in this, the harshest aporia of the *Parmenides* (133b). Aristotle himself says explicitly that there is a basic reason for postulating the ideas: in view of the ever shifting tides of appearances, everything hinges on knowledge of their ideas if there is to be any knowledge at all (*Metaphysics* 987a32 ff.). Surely the entire doctrine of the ideas rests upon an obvious assumption: one cannot take the chōrismos to mean that the connection presupposed [between the ideas and appearances] is now to be severed.

One need only keep in mind what Plato had in view and the historical motivation that led him to carry out this separation of the ideas from appearances. Before him lay the entire expanse of the mathematical sciences. There is hardly a better characterization of the fact that Euclidean geometry refers to pure spatial relationships—and not to the sensory images of a circle or triangle that we draw as illustrations—than its requirement that mathematical constructs be separated from the sensory world. And one cannot even say that the distinction here is all too self-evident. Pythagorean mathematics was certainly genuine mathematics, and its theorems and proofs obviously did not refer to the figures produced to illustrate them. But plainly it had no appropriate understanding of how its true objects—circle, triangle, number—differ from sense perceptions. This lack of understanding is portrayed explicitly in Plato's *Theaetetus*, and corresponding to it there existed at this time the practice of mathematical pseudo-proof, which adduced the way things seem to the eyes, for example, the coincidence of a straight line with a very slightly curved segment of a circle, in support of its 'mathematical' argumentation. Only the ontological divorce of the noetic from the sensory, which is to say, Plato's chōrismos, cleared things up sufficiently in this regard for mathematicians to be able to say what they were dealing with, and to make evident that what they were doing was in any case not some sort of physics. This distinction between mathematics and physics is a fundamental truth. Moreover, it is no coincidence that modern mathematical natural science can make a lot more sense of Plato's treatment of the world of mathematics as an intelligible reality for itself and as a prefiguration of nature than it can of Aristotle's derivation of the world of mathematical objects by abstraction (*aphairesis*) from physical appearances. Aristotle's 'solution' (*Physics*, Beta 2) suppresses the actual problem of the being of what is mathematical, which is to say, that very being-for-itself which has such seminal relationships to the being of appearances as those discovered by modern mathematical physics and anticipated by Plato in the *Timaeus*.[14]

Things are similar in regard to moral phenomena. The distinction between justice itself and what is considered (*dokei*) to be just is anything but an empty conceptual abstraction. On the contrary, it is the truth of our practical consciousness itself, the truth as Plato saw it graphically before his own eyes in the person of Socrates: true and just human behavior cannot be based on the conventional concepts and standards to which public opinion clings. Rather, such behavior must take as its standard only those norms that transcend any question of public acceptance, and even the question of whether they can be, or are ever found to be, fully realized, and that thereby display themselves to our moral consciousness as incontestably and unalterably true and right. This severance of the noetic from the sensory, of true insight from mere points of view—this chōrismos, in other words—is the truth of moral consciousness as such. Again, it is no coincidence that this insight of Plato's was dignified anew

14. Compare my "Dialetic and Sophism in Plato's *Seventh Letter*" and "Idea and Reality in Plato's *Timaeus*."

when the concern was to give morality a transcendental foundation. Kant's rigor is exceeded only by the rigor with which Plato,
in the dialogue on the true state, compels his Socrates to separate
the true essence of morality from what is held to be socially acceptable (*Republic*, book 2) and to display this separation with
the example of a man who is held by all to be unjust and therefore put to death by use of every conceivable torture (361c ff.).

And finally, what if one now ventures out upon the entire vast
sea of the things we say and looks for a fixed orientation within
the ups and downs of speaking and reflection, amidst the very
unsteadiness, in other words, which had been cultivated at just
that time into the new art of speaking and arguing that Plato de-
rogatorily labels sophism?[15] Once again, only the divorce of the
illusory way an argument sounds from its real meaning and of
the apparent cogency of what is said from the consequential
logic inherent in the subject matter can provide that orientation.
The so-called epistemological excursus of the *Seventh Letter*
(which I have already treated elsewhere[16]) makes completely
clear, I think, what this divorce actually means. It is intended to
expose the weakness of sense experience, a weakness that threatens to prevent our reaching any mutual understanding.[17]

The chōrismos is not a doctrine that must first be overcome.

15. That the label was discriminatory, at least in the eyes of high society, is
demonstrated by the *Protagoras* 317b.

16. See "Dialectic and Sophism in Plato's *Seventh Letter*."

17. In his "Dialectic and Sophism in Plato's *Seventh letter*," Gadamer shows
how the "means" of language—name, image, concept, idea—can all assert
themselves instead of the thing that they were intended to bring to light. Thus
language, as that which "lets things be" (Heidegger), conceals as well as dis-
closes: Sophism is quick to seize upon this potential of language to obfuscate and
confuse, for its concern is not with the truth but with manipulation. The "new
paideia," to which Gadamer often refers, was essentially instruction in the techniques of manipulation by means of language. TRANSLATOR.

Rather, from beginning to end, it is an essential component of true dialectic. Dialectic, consequently, is not to be advanced as evidence against the chōrismos and is not a remedy for it. That Aristotle focuses his critique on the issue of the chōrismos even so must be understood in reference to the point he wishes to make in opposition to Plato, that is, in reference to his emphasis on physics and the ontological primacy of a given particular. And in any case, his attack on the chōrismos cannot represent a total break with the fundamental orientation of Plato's thought toward the logoi. The question of just what Aristotle's critique meant within Plato's school and among Platonists will always have to be raised anew, it seems, and in order to raise it a comprehensive elaboration of the underlying accord between Aristotle's and Plato's doctrines of the *logos tou eidous* (statement of the form) and of what these doctrines have in common, would be required here. Only in this way could the ground be cleared for a meaningful articulation of Aristotle's divergent doctrine.

The following investigation concentrates on the problem of the idea of the good. The idea of the good is not just any one idea among all the others; rather, in Plato's view too, it occupies a preeminent place. I shall attempt to work out what its special status is and to shed new light on the importance of that special status for the fundamental problem in Platonism—which is just as much the fundamental problem in Aristotle *that is, the role of the eidetic entities, or forms*. Here we are in a privileged position with regard to the indirect tradition, since Aristotle deals at length in all his ethical treatises with the question of the good, or the *megiston mathēma* (most important insight) as Plato had designated it. So perhaps in the mirror of Aristotle's critique we can also acquire the key to why the ideas were introduced in the first place. There is a common theme in Plato and Aristotle here. This fact, which alone makes possible any evaluation of Aristotle's critique of Plato, has been neglected in modern scholarship until now because of the dominant "historical" interpretive schema deriving from Hegel *that construes its subject matter in terms of* antithetical relationships. Scholarship, it seems to me, finds itself at a loss in regard to Aristotle's critique of Plato as a consequence of this neglect. I see the beginnings of a better understanding of this critique in Anglo-American research, for example, in Cherniss's *The Riddle of the Platonic Academy*— which in my views gets somewhat bogged down, nonetheless, in arguing against the traditionally accepted authority of Aristotle's accounts—and in Lee's *Phronēsis*.[18] Each rightly relies on, and emphasizes, the dialectical, propaedeutical character of the critical introductory books in Aristotle's three ethical treatises. But to do that is not enough. The task is to get back to the common ground upon which both Plato and Aristotle base their talk of the eidos.

The question about the good and, in particular, about the good in the sense of aretē, the "best-ness" of the citizen of the *polis* (city-state), dominates Plato's writings from the very start. And even if we leave aside the consensus that has been reached today regarding the chronology of Plato's dialogues by and large, there can be no doubt that in these writings the doctrine of the ideas does not occur in the same way from beginning to end. Naturally that does not mean that Plato came to this theory only later on. It is time that we finally abandoned such a naive chron-

18. Cf. H. F. Cherniss, *The Riddle of the Platonic Academy* (Berkeley, 1945), and E. N. Lee, "Exegesis and Argument," in *Phronēsis*, vol. 1 (1973). Only after I had completed this manuscript did two books appear that show that I am not alone in my contention: A. Blum, *Theorizing* (London, 1974), and above all, J. Findlay's thorough and speculative work, *Plato. The Written and Unwritten Doctrines* (London, 1974), my review of which has appeared in the meantime in the *Philosophische Rundshau*, vol. 24 (1977).

ological ordering of Plato's dialogical fiction, which in the end was tantamount to a veritable game of running back and forth from one home base to another. Instead, we shall seek structural similarities among groups of dialogues, so that along the way we may clarify both Plato's intentions as an author as well as the implicit content of the dialogues.

Consequently, we shall distinguish among the different types of dialogue in Plato's works, *and once these have been identified,* we will be able to establish a structural chronology based upon them. The "aporetic" dialogues, in which Socrates refutes his interlocutors without finally giving an answer to the question posed, represent one clearly defined type of Socratic discussion. (Given Xenophon's apologetical efforts to bring out the positive side of Socrates' art of refutation, there is no real correlation between this type and what the "para-tradition" in Xenophon tells us, nor between this type of dialogue and the pseudo-Platonic(?) *Clitopho*. Still, these very apologetical tendencies in Xenophon do provide a certain indirect confirmation of the historical Socrates' "negativity" [just by denying it].) The new role that Socrates plays in the discussion of the just state [in the *Republic*], for instance, should, and must, be perceived as a clearly accentuated change. Socrates talks virtually the whole night long, and there is certainly no lack of bold positivity in his utopia. Furthermore, the affinity in the content and themes of the discussions in the "negative" [or aporetic] dialogues unifies them as a group. All the refutations which they contain of the preconceptions about aretē that the interlocutors bring with them to the discussion—be they young people, their fathers, or the celebrated sophist teachers of the time—have a common character: no answer is found to the questions posed, namely, what this or that aretē actually is, or whether aretē can be taught or not, in view of the unclarity and deceptiveness of whatever particular thing is taken to be aretē [piety, courage, and so forth].

In contrast, the inclusiveness of the question posed in the *Republic* seems intended to counter the conventionality of the conceptions of aretē found in the earlier discussions. Here the inquiry is about the *sympasa aretē* (all-encompassing virtue) and *dikaiosynē* (justice), and consequently about all aretai (virtues). And at the end the idea of the good "beyond" all these is introduced. The knowledge sought is not there, and perhaps is not even attainable, as long as one does not consciously look beyond what is generally accepted to be knowledge. *In assessing just how far we have gone beyond the Socratic dialogues here*, it is of particular significance that Plato's brothers are the ones who make the transition with Socrates in the discussion in book 2 of the *Republic.*

The key notion in what is generally accepted to be knowledge is technē (art). For Plato too, that goes without saying. Thus, in the *Apology*, Socrates finds among the handworkers, at least, real knowledge of the special things they deal with. To be sure, like other "wise" men, handworkers, too, fail us when the concern is the most important thing of all (*ta megista*) (*Apology* 22d), for which all human will to know ultimately strives. Knowledge of the good is exactly what is not asked about in the technai (arts) and by the *technitēs* (artisan-handworker). That it is not is the standard argument used later by Aristotle in his critique of Plato (*Nicomachean Ethics* 1097a5 ff., henceforth *EN; Eudemian Ethics* 1218b2, henceforth *EE; Magna Moralia* 1182b25 ff., henceforth *MM*). But this fact, far from weighing against Plato, is precisely what gets Plato's Socrates started on his way. His awareness of it is the basis of his superior "ignorance." Knowledge of the good would seem to be different in kind from all familiar human knowledge. Hence, if measured against such a concept of specialized expertise, it could indeed be called ignorance. The *anthrōpinē sophia* (human wisdom) that is aware of such ignorance must inquire beyond, and see beyond, all the widespread presumed knowledge that Plato later will call "*doxa*" (belief, opinion). That the good can be caught sight of only in this *apoblepein pros*—this looking at it in seeing past all else—is not merely suggested by the negative result of the Socratic discussions. It is stated explicitly in the first dialogue in which the acceptance of the ideas is actually proposed, the *Phaedo*. The *Phaedo* thus stands as the noteworthy link between the elenchtic or refutational dialogues, which must be attributed to the early Plato, and his work on the ideal state.

The *Phaedo* has been singled out as the dialogue in which Plato first introduces us to the doctrine of the ideas. The Marburg school in particular availed itself of Plato's introduction of eidos as the best "hypothesis," for a somewhat forced assimilation of Plato to Kant. To be sure, Natorp's interpretation was not lacking in insight into the exceptional role of the good. For him the good was the principle of self-preservation. He saw hypothesizing the eidos as a procedure for knowing this principle, and in this way he came to identify "idea" with "natural law." What he had in mind, accordingly, was natural science. In its ascending hypotheses the latter does indeed move ever closer to the true order of the universe, and it is carried out in ongoing determination of its object. For Natorp the "thing in itself" is nothing more than the infinite, "unending task."

Today that interpretation sounds like false modernism. If, instead, one looks at the *Phaedo* as an interim stage on the way to the idea of the *good*, another structural parallel emerges. After all, the *Phaedo* too is a dialogue full of refutations, and in their own way the interlocutors in the *Phaedo* represent a position that is to be taken seriously, even if they defend it only halfheartedly, namely, "scientifically" founded materialism. They are Pythagoreans, of course, but Pythagoreans of a later generation that is entirely at home in mathematics and science and that ab-

jures the contemporary sophistic argumentation as such. Thus
they have become Socrates' friends. It turns out that for them the
religious background of Pythagoreanism has faded away entirely. The "inner plot" of the dialogue consists precisely in the
demonstration to these Pythagoreans of the true consequences of
their own thinking—consequences that point to the "idea."
Thus at one and the same time their understanding of themselves
as "materialists" is refuted, and their mathematical idealism
confirmed.[19]

Aristotle introduces Plato precisely as a Pythagorean (*Metaphysics*, Alpha 6), but it is not only in retrospect from Aristotle
that it becomes clear that these Pythagoreans in the *Phaedo* are,
in a certain sense, very close to Plato's thinking. The further we
penetrate into the problems surrounding Plato's development of
a doctrine of an *archē*—problems that first appear in the late dialogues, in particular in the *Philebus*—the more evident it becomes that the Pythagorean position represents the real link
between the insoluble problems *Plato displays* in this new
technē-based paideia and his later dialectic. It is no accident that
the question of the "invisible" *psychē* (soul) is the vehicle first
chosen to exemplify the "invisible" noetic dimension of mathematics and the ideas. Seeking the *koinon pasi agathon* (the good
common to all things), Socrates turned to Anaxagoras's treatise
in the expectation of finding it in the latter's concept of *nous* (intellection, mind). And when, perplexed and disappointed, he finally sees himself forced to hypothesize the eidos in order to
get clear about the true sense of "*aitia*" (cause) in all things
(100a–c), he takes the approach of mathematical illustrations.
But in the end it becomes fully clear that only looking to what is
good (*apoblepein pros ton agathon*), or to what is better or best,

19. Cf. my study, "The Proofs of Immortality in Plato's *Phaedo*."

respectively, promises him real knowledge, or, as we would say, "understanding"—understanding, namely, of the universe as well as the polis and the psyche. To this extent the work on the polis [the *Republic*] (which is every bit as much on the psyche) and then, later, the *Timaeus*, adhere to, and articulate, the program projected in the *Phaedo's* flight into the logoi (statements).

It is not in the least excessive to see in Aristotle's textbooks the execution of just this project, particularly in his *Physics* and his *Politics*, which contains his ethics. We have here an ideal of science which plainly did not impede the birth and astonishing development of the Hellenistic specialized sciences. For modern natural science, on the other hand, that Aristotelian ideal represented the antagonist: it was dogmatic, teleological anthropomorphism that had to be overcome. All attempts to renew this ideal of a teleological, homogeneous science, beginning with Leibniz and continuing through the Romantic philosophy of nature to thinkers like Whitehead, have been unable to assert themselves against the inexorable, step-by-step progress of the modern experimental sciences. Precisely the failure of these attempts, however, indirectly confirms that reason has need of unity—a need that underlies the Socratic requirement. And it is from just this need that the claim of universality in the doctrine of the ideas derives.[20]

20. The point to which Gadamer often returns in this work is that for Plato and Aristotle the good could function simultaneously as an ontological-theoretical, as well as a practical, concept, indeed, that these two realms remained continuous. As the *Phaedo* makes clear, natural processes were to be grasped theoretically as purposive, as tending toward what is good. Aristotle's teleology merely extends this way of thinking. Consequently, for both Plato and Aristotle, human practice—making choices for the sake of what is good, better, or best, respectively—occurs within the setting of the cosmos. Modern science, which rejects teleology as anthropomorphism, leads to a severance of theoretical science from practice and of theoretical reason from practical reason. Reason as such, which seeks unity in its enterprises, naturally rebels once that happens.

In this regard the idea of the good assumes a special significance within Plato's new noetic orientation. The *Republic* focuses on it, and it provides the basis for determining the order of
the polis and the psychē. Socrates' partners in the discussion
would be content if he were to speak about the good in the same
way as he had spoken earlier about dikaiosynē (justice) and *sō-*
phrosynē (temperance) (*Republic* 506d). But whenever the conversation turns to this highest and ultimate subject, the speaker
in Plato begs off, saying that it would be unnecessary at that moment to go into it and perhaps even beyond his abilities—just as
in the *Timaeus* at 48a, for instance. And as a matter of fact, the
famous epekeina tēs ousias (beyond all being) lends the idea of
the good a transcendence that distinguishes it from all other noetic objects, which is to say all other ideas.

That Plato uses only the word *idea*, and never *eidos*, for the
agathon, surely has something to do with that transcendence.
There is no denying, of course, that these words, *idea* and *eidos*,
were interchangeable in the Greek of that time and in the language usage of the philosophers too. Still, that Plato never
speaks of the *eidos tou agathou* (form of the good) indicates that
the idea of the good has a character all its own. *Eidos* always refers only to the object, as accords with its being neuter. In following the natural tendency of our thinking to objectify, the

---

Though Gadamer does not pursue the thought here, one might add that the
contemporary pseudo-scientific forms of "moral reasoning," utilitarianism in
particular, also confirm reason's need for unity insofar as they aim to carry the
scientific method over into the realm of practice, and thereby reestablish the
unity of reason. But here the result is the evisceration of moral thought. A.
MacIntyre, in *After Virtue* (Notre Dame, 1980), shows convincingly why such
attempts inevitably miscarry and end in "emotivism." In so doing, he corrobo-
rates Gadamer's argument that the methodology of modern natural science is
misplaced in many fields of the human quest for truth—in aesthetic interpretation, politics, history, and, not least of all, moral philosophy. TRANSLATOR.

feminine form, *idea*, can certainly designate an object too, as do *doxa* and *epistēmē*. But in *idea*, taken as a "view of something," the viewing or looking is more pronounced than in *eidos*, taken as "how something looks." Consequently *idea tou agathou* (idea of the good) implies not so much the "view of the good" as a "looking to the good," as numerous turns of speech such as *apoblepein pros* show.

In any case, in the *Republic* Socrates treats the idea of the good as something that is difficult to grasp and that can be observed only in its effects. Like the sun, which by granting warmth and light, gives everything visible its being and perceptibility, the good is present for us only in the gifts that it bestows, *gnōsis kai alētheia*, insight and truth. It would seem futile to want to grasp the good directly and know it like some *mathēma* (learned insight), for the very nature of it appears to preclude this possibility. To begin with, its ineffability, its being *arrēton* (unsayable), should be interpreted as soberly as possible. To say that is by no means to deny that the religious background of Greek thought is discernible here. Thanks to the expositions of Gerhard Krüger, we know that it is.[21] But one should be aware that Plotinus takes a new step when he also calls the "One" *epekeina noēseōs* (beyond all thinking), and when he takes all being and all thinking too as a pointer into transcendence. In the context of the *Republic*, in contrast, the good is presented as the unifying one of the many. In other words, the good is articulated precisely in respect to the inner duality and dialectical function of the one which Plotinus's double "beyond" [beyond being (*ousia*) and beyond thought (*noēsis*)] is specifically intended to exclude.[22]

21. G. Krüger, *Einsicht und Leidenschaft. Das Wesen des platonischen Denkens* (Frankfurt, 1948).

22. Gadamer's argument, which he elaborates in "Plato's Unwritten Dialectic," is that Plato is distorted in the Plotinian reading of him insofar as the ines-

Now there seems to be a simple way to account for this privileged status and incomprehensibility of the idea of the good, which distinguishes it from the remaining ideas. The idea of the good, it is said, is precisely what comes "first" (*to prōton*), and is thus removed from any derivation. Thus it is what one was later to call a principle. And, after all, this solution has generally been the one resorted to ever since Aristotle, who was the first to introduce the concept of the *archē* (first principle). Furthermore, wherever Aristotle introduces Plato's philosophy as an extension of Pythagorean teachings, he does in fact treat it as analogous to the Pythagorean doctrine of the peras (limit), and the apeiron (unlimited, indefinite). He presents it in the doctrine of the *hen* (one) and the *ahoristos dyas* (indeterminate two)—the two principles of either the ideas or ideal numbers, as the case may be. It seems consistent to grant the idea of the good in Plato the same special place that Aristotle assigned to those two principles in his account, for it would explain why any speaking of the idea of the good, which is to say, all dialectical treatment of it, could never take "the good itself" as its object directly, and why, conse-

---

capable concomitance (Heidegger: *Gleichursprünglichkeit*) of unity and indeterminate duality is lost from view. It is far more accurate, he contends, to see Plato's number doctrine as an extension of *both* the Pythagorean concepts: the peras and the apeiron too. For Plato, whatever is unified or delimited as "one" finds itself within the indeterminate duality (*ahoristos dyas*) of unlimited extremes, for example, large and small, hot and cold, pleasure and pain, and so forth. Hence what is determined as one, as *a* thing, is inseparable from the indeterminacy in which it is embedded.

This point has important consequences for Plato's ethical thought as Gadamer understands it: human beings are never purely good, which is to say never purely harmonized, integral, unified, but always struggling for (*diamachesthai*) unity against those passions and drives that threaten them with dissolution and loss of integrity. It is in this sense that Plato's ethics may be said to be "dialectical": reasonableness (*nous, phronēsis*) is always in dialectical tension with the immediate desire for what is "sweet" (*hēdonē*). TRANSLATOR.

quently, whenever Plato fixes his sights on it, he does so in the
language of analogy.

Convincing corroboration of this point comes to light in the
Philebus. Of course there the concern at first is not the idea of
the good but the question of the good in human life. But in the
end, any talk about the universal idea of the good always takes
as its point of departure this *human* question: What is the good
for us? That this is the case emerges clearly in Socrates' self-
portrayal in the *Phaedo*. The particular question raised in the
Philebus is the extent to which the passion of our drives and our
consciousness while thinking can be harmoniously balanced in
life. Putting the question this way implies turning from the realm
of the ideal to what is best in reality—which appears to run directly counter to the *Republic's* project of constructing the ideal
state. But there, too, this turn to the practical is not altogether
unheard of. To start with, the *Republic* also addresses the good
in human life, for it opens with the very same question as the
Philebus, namely, whether the good is *hēdonē* (pleasure), as the
mass of people (*hoi polloi*) believe, or phronēsis (reason), that is,
whether it consists in satisfaction of one's vital drives or insight
into the good (*Republic* 505b). Of course, here in the *Philebus*
this antithesis is no longer stated as a clear-cut either-or. Har-
monizing and balancing the two sides has been elevated to the
central concern.

This shift, we can say, makes human practice the theme, and
alongside of this consideration of the practical, a physics can
now be placed, of which the *Philebus* also gives preliminary indications and upon which the mythical narrative of the *Timaeus*
discourses. After all, both these dialogues are directed to the
realm of genesis (becoming), and in a way that contrasts funda-
mentally with Plato's sharp separation of being and becoming.
Nevertheless, in the *Timaeus* especially, this separation provides

the framework that sustains the dialogue, just as it does in the *Republic*. Thus the actual question in the *Timaeus* remains the same, namely, how we are to think of chōrismos and methexis in combination with each other.

The relationship between the two comes into focus even more clearly in the *Philebus* than it does in the ideal celestial mathematics and terrestrial physics of the *Timaeus*. In the *Philebus* the idea of the good has precisely the function of providing practical orientation for the right and just life insofar as this life is a mixture of pleasure and knowing and insofar as the mixing of this life, which is described at the conclusion, is explicitly said to be regulated by the idea of measure, measuredness, rationality—or however else one might epitomize all the structural determinations of the beautiful in whose appearances alone the good itself is to be comprehended. From Aristotle, and above all from the subsequent accounts of philosophers' teachings, it would appear to follow that the good can simply be called the one, and the one the good. The fact that it can does not seriously conflict with what the dialogues say. For this "one" is certainly not Plotinus's "One," the sole existent and "trans-existent" entity. Rather, it is that which on any given occasion provides what is multiple with the unity of whatever consists in itself. As the unity of what is unitary, the idea of the good would seem to be presupposed by anything ordered, enduring, and consistent. That means, however, that it is presupposed as the unity of many. When we make this fact our starting point, we get our first sense of the paradigmatic function of the arithmos (number) structure, a structure that plays a decisive role in the indirect tradition's account of Plato. The number, after all, is also unity and multiplicity simultaneously. That it is both is illustrated in particular by the fact that for the Greeks "one" was not an arithmos, that is, not a sum, not a unity of many. Rather, it was the constitutive element of the numbers. The smallest arithmos is the "two," and thus any number must already be precisely a multiplicity and a unity at the same time.[23] In any event, the idea of the good does not seem to be a supreme mathēma to which every other sort of knowledge (*technē*), all practical knowing and all physics alike, would be subordinate, and which could be known and learned as these are.

23. Compare my work on "Plato's Unwritten Dialectic."

I I

SOCRATIC KNOWING
AND NOT-KNOWING

Our preliminary review of the special place of the good in Plato's thinking about the ideas has shown us that Plato himself saw that knowledge of the good cannot be understood using technē as a model, although—or better said, precisely because— Socrates continually uses this technē model in his critique and refutation of the views of his partners in the discussion. If one brings Aristotle's illuminating analyses of the modes of knowing (*hexeis tou alētheuein*) (*EN*, book 4) to bear on this insight, and in particular his differentiation between technical and practical knowledge, the end result is not even surprising: we see how close the knowledge of the good sought by Socrates is to Aristotle's phronēsis. In treating phronēsis, Aristotle explicitly distinguishes practical knowledge from both theoretical and technical knowledge.[1] He characterizes it as a different kind of knowing

---

1. Plato's efforts to distinguish Socratic moral reasoning from the new technē of sophism are of particular interest to Gadamer insofar as in *WM* he attempts to show that there are forms of reasoning and of giving justification that are quite different from those of natural science and technology. In this book he shows that technical or scientific expertise, if carried over into the moral sphere, becomes an amoral, if not immoral, art of achieving success in the pursuit of pleasure. Again, modern utilitarianism (see chapter 1, n. 20) and post-utilitarian contractualism, however well-intentioned, would open the gates to sophism if Gadamer is right. For these are attempts to carry scientific, methodical reasoning over into ethics. J. Rawls, for instance, in *A Theory of Justice* (Cambridge, 1972) p. 121, goes so far as to speak of a "moral geometry." TRANSLATOR.

(*allo eidos gnōseōs*) (*EN* 1141b33, 1142a30; *EE* 1246b36). The virtue of practical knowledge, of phronēsis, appears as the epitome of everything that Socrates' exemplary life displays. The picture of Socrates that Plato draws in the *Apology* also shows him to be far removed from any merely "theoretical" concern.

Nevertheless, elsewhere in Plato things look quite different, and he forces upon his Socrates figure far more complex roles— the antagonist in his dramas, for instance, to sophist paideia, and, in addition, the enthusiast for myth who tells us of bizarre realms lying somewhere between religious fables and philosophical thought, and, above all, the dialectician who broadens his own art of leading a discussion into a paradigm for all cognition and truth. Here Socrates becomes a mythical figure in whom knowledge of the good ultimately coalesces with knowledge of the true and knowledge of being in a highest theōria as it were. Our task originates here: it is to raise this mythical unity of knowledge of the good, the true, and the real to the level of conceptual thinking, and in so doing, to make comprehensible what Aristotle shares with Plato even when he critically separates himself from him.

It is characteristic and significant that Plato himself consistently delimits knowledge of the good from all other knowledge only in a negative way. In the Socratic dialogues he elaborates the difference by sovereignly reducing the discussion to an aporia. Whoever thinks he knows what aretē is, is refuted. And it is always taken for granted that it is the standard of the technai by which his "knowledge" is to be measured. It turns out that each one of those questioned lacks knowledge of the good. Of course, when Plato's Socrates, be it in the *Phaedo* or the *Republic*, goes on to speak of passing beyond everything else knowable in moving toward knowledge of the good, and when he singles out the good because of its transcendence, he does tie the argument into the Socratic question about the virtues and the resultant question about the good. But, imperceptibly, Plato's Socrates proceeds here to a theoretical knowledge of the good and of being. What he calls dialectic is a sort of meta-science that opens up behind the mathematical disciplines described here as pure theoretical sciences.

Nevertheless, this science is not called "dialectic" unthinkingly. The heritage of Socrates and his art of dialogue lives on in it. Accordingly, Plato often applies the word phronēsis—which for Aristotle characterizes the virtue of practical reasonableness—in a wide sense. And he can also use it as synonymous with both technē and epistēmē. This usage is never meant to imply that knowledge of the good is really the kind of knowledge that technē is. [Rather, it shows that] the knowledge of the handworker plays such a paradigmatic role in any kind of knowing at all that language usage conforms to it. Besides, there is indeed something that practical reason and technical know-how have in common: in a certain sense it is true of anyone who has a science or art that his knowledge is based on grounds, reasons. That holds for the doctor (an example of which Aristotle is particularly fond), for the mathematician, and for anyone at all who claims to have knowledge as opposed to mere opinion.

Still, an essential difference between technical-theoretical reasonableness and practical reasonableness becomes discernible here at once. When he who knows is required to give reasons in any other case but practical matters, he can draw upon a general knowledge that he has learned. It is exactly this recourse to general knowledge that characterizes technē or epistēmē. Hence, in regard to these Plato speaks of a mathēma (an insight to be learned). But things look very different in respect to the exercise of practical reason. Here one cannot rely upon previously acquired general knowledge, and yet one still claims to reach a judgment by one's own weighing of the pros and cons and to decide reasonably in each case. Whoever deliberates with himself and with others about what would be the right thing to do in a particular practical situation is plainly prepared to support his decision with nothing other than good reasons,[2] and he who always behaves this reasonably possesses the virtue of reasonableness, of "well-advised-ness." (*Euboulia* was a political slogan of the new paideia of that time.) Now it strikes me as significant

2. Gadamer is raising the issue here of moral argumentation, that is, how I can justify to myself and others the choices that I make at the end of my moral deliberations. Giving justification—*logon didonai*—means giving grounds, or reasons, in support of my decision. In a society such as that in which Socrates finds himself, a society, namely, in which "no one does what is just voluntarily," the mere patterning of one's behavior on paragons of virtue no longer suffices. (See "Plato and the Poets" and "Plato's Educational State.") And appeals to traditional morality become empty rationalizations of self-interest. Consequently, one must take a stand and be able to hold to it—to justify it. The issue then becomes what sort of justification this will be, for it is clear that giving reasons, or grounds, in scientific accounts of things is quite different. What the difference is emerges clearly in regard to teaching and learning. Scientific knowledge and technical know-how can be taught. What is right, just, or good, on the other hand, cannot.

With that we come to a critical question for Gadamer. On the one hand, he argues that we are dependent on tradition for justifying our moral choices and places great emphasis on *Sitten*, or moral customs (see *WM* 11). The authority of these alone, and not autonomous intellection, founds our morality. On the other hand, he emphasizes here that Socrates, as an individual, knows a good that transcends the merely "conventional" morality to which *hoi polloi*, or the "many" (Heidegger: *das Man*), uncritically subscribe. This apparent contradiction could be resolved, I suggest, if one were to distinguish between traditional, as opposed to conventional, morality. The latter, though its sophist advocates often appeal to traditional authorities (Homer and the like) for justification, consists in fact of nothing more than prudential accommodations coerced and acceded to, respectively, by unequal individuals whose sense of solidarity and community with each other has vanished. What is convened on here is not what is *sittlich*, but what is convenient for the most powerful. Here, might indeed makes right, and no real justification is possible (cf. *Republic*, books 1 and 2). TRANSLATOR.

that Plato holds fast to this characteristic of practical knowledge, and that he distances himself from technical knowledge. Dialectic is not general and teachable knowledge, even if Plato often follows customary language usage and also speaks of it as technē or epistēme. It is not in the least surprising, however, that he can call dialectic "phronēsis" too. Dialectic is not something that one can simply learn. It is more than that. It is "reasonableness."

Plainly, in calling dialectic "phronēsis," Plato is again following a language usage in which it is perfectly natural to give that name to the aretē proper to human dealings. That fact comes out most clearly in the *Meno*, 88b ff.[3] This passage is of particular interest because Socrates, here in the midst of one of his didactic speeches, is astonishingly conciliatory. He does not insist at all on a complete equation of virtue with knowledge. He leaves open the question of whether other things besides phronēsis pertain to aretē: ". . . *phronēsis ara phamen aretēn einai ētoi sympasan ē meros ti*" (we say then that phronēsis is aretē, be it either the whole of it or a part). Obviously his point is only that, whatever the case may be, phronēsis plays a role. Aristotle himself says exactly that in book 6 and the *Nicomachean Ethics* (1144b17 ff.).

From this observation one may conclude that Aristotle remains true to the actual language usage of *phronēsis* in his ethics, as in fact he does generally. It is not the case, as Natorp believed, that Aristotle restricted a ceremonious artificial word of Plato's to the ethical realm. Quite the reverse: Plato in fact widened the

3. The way in which the aretē of *phronēsai* (being reasonable) is distinguished from the so-called aretai of the psychē at *Republic* 518e provides a nice illustration of the main meaning that is to be heard in *phronēsis* and which Xenophon always has in mind. Compare, too, the *Symposium* 209a: *Phronēsin te kai tēn allēn aretēn* (*phronēsis* and the other virtue) and similar passages.

customary usage, whose proximity to practice must have always been sensed,[4] to include dialectical knowing, and he did so in order to ceremoniously exalt dialectic. In other words, he took what was called practical reasonableness and expanded it to include the theoretical disposition of the dialectician.

Conversely, if on occasion Aristotle himself follows Plato's widened language usage, one should not overburden this circumstance by basing hypotheses about Aristotle's "development" on it, as Jaeger, Walzer, and others once tried to do. In truth, it demonstrates only that Aristotle continues to live in the same word of language as Plato's. Nor does it in any way mean that in such cases Aristotle forgot the proper sense of *phronēsis*— whose meaning he himself analyzed—or that he was consciously "Platonizing." By the same token, however, the use of *phronēsis* in Plato himself does indicate that he was aiming at something common to both practical and theoretical knowing that transcends the distinction between them. Precisely this may have been his motive for broadening the usage of *phronēsis* to include the highest form of knowing: he wants to assign to the true dialectician not a mere skill, but real reasonableness. At the same time, this distinction implies that for Plato the dialectician does not possess some superior art, which he employs in *self*-justification,[5] but that, instead, he seeks real justification. Hence he does not possess an art that he uses whenever he so desires. Dialectic

4. Compare Shnell's recent exhaustive investigation of Homer's use of *phronēsis* in *Glotta* 55 (1977): 32–64.

5. *Rechthaben*; the allusion here is to the sophist's desire always "to be in the right." In "Dialectic and Sophism in Plato's *Seventh Letter*," Gadamer points out that for Plato self-assertiveness and obduracy are among the chief obstacles in the pursuit of the truth: precisely because a belief is mine, I tend to cling to it rather than permit myself to be shown that it is false. Sophism only reinforces this propensity insofar as it gives me the means of confounding any counterargument to my contention. TRANSLATOR.

is not so much a technē—that is, an ability and knowledge—as a way of being.[6] It is a disposition, or *hexis* in Aristotle's sense of the word, that distinguishes the genuine philosopher from the sophist. To be sure, it will take some doing to defend this distinction to the advocates of the new paideia. The pivotal reason why dialectic is only dialectic—that is, a process of giving and receiving justification, and not knowledge like that of a handworker or knowledge in the so-called sciences—is plainly that talk which confuses and confounds does not constitute a threat in both these other realms in the same way that it threatens inquiry into the good. It may certainly be said of technē, and epistēmē too, that they know, that is, that they have reasons for proceeding in this way or that or for holding this or that to be true. Socrates' questioning of the handworkers in the *Apology* shows this knowledge to be characteristic of each of them in their specialties. Once the handworkers have learned their trade, they know why they do what they do and how they do it, and in any event, their knowledge is displayed in the fact that they know how to teach their art. Within their competencies they are not to be shaken by the sophistic arts of rhetoric and argumentation, and a figure such as Hippias, who passes himself off as some sort of

6. Something of the early Heidegger can be detected here, in particular his contrasting of authenticity and inauthenticity (cf. *Sein und Zeit* (Tübingen, 1960] henceforth *SZ*). Philosophers not only think differently, they exist differently—differently from *das Man* (everybody), or, as Plato would say, hoi polloi (the many). They are differently disposed insofar as they hold to what is true. The decisive passage in Plato is *Theatetus* 174a ff., where the otherworldliness of the philosopher is portrayed from the viewpoint of hoi polloi: he appears hopelessly inept and is mocked by maidservants (and sophists). In his lectures at Boston College, Gadamer pointed out that in fact Thales would not have fallen into the well, as the maidservant presumed (174b), but would have climbed down in order to view the stars without the interference of peripheral light. A contemporary reader of Plato would have understood just whom Plato is portraying as ignorant here—not Thales, but self-proclaimed "practical" people. TRANSLATOR.

expert at everything, is not likely to have impressed any handworker.

The knowledge of the doctor or the mathematician is also secure in the same way. We know that the new paideia tried to create confusion with its techniques here too. In the case of the medical art, after all, it can play upon a general suspicion that arises again and again, given the limits of medical skills and the impossibility of medicine's proving that it is responsible for its successes. Are we really dealing with a science here? The tract *Peri Technēs (On Technē)* which comes from the era of sophism, gives us a good idea of this vulnerability. Something like it exists even in the knowledge of the mathematician, who, as we can also easily understand, is vexed on occasion by the intransigence of everyday experience. We know that to a large extent Protagoras devoted his rhetorical arts to discrediting the mathematician.[7] Since the subject matter in mathematics tends not to be grasped as readily as the subject matter of handwork, it is all the easier to understand why he did so. It may also be true that the mathematician himself is incapable of exposing the false impression that such deliberately confusing arts of argumentation give. However, the *Theatetus* dialogue, which speaks to just this predicament, confirms at the same time how a real mathematician would respond. Theodorus and Theatetus remain immune to such arguments and simply steer clear of them (see *Theatetus* 164e, 169c). They see what they are dealing with—numbers or figures—as if these were there before their eyes. Knowing is the immediacy of having something before one's eyes in this way, and therefore it can be called "aisthēsis" (perception).

The situation is very different, however, where there is no specialized knowing and no specialists, and where, nevertheless,

7. H. Diels, *Fragmente der Vorsokratiker*, vol. 2 (Berlin, 1907), p. 266.

each one of us must have the right to his own opinion. I am referring to the question of the good in personal, as well as social, life.
Here everybody talks to everybody else, and each seeks to convince the other of the veracity of his opinion, especially when it
comes to political decisions. A debate about the good is always
going on, and as we saw, everyone would maintain that he was
doing nothing other than advancing reasons or grounds. The
claim made by the new paideia is founded on this circumstance,
in particular the claim it makes for its rhetoric, which is really
the new art. We see this foundation most clearly in the way that
Protagoras defends this claim for his rhetoric in Plato's dialogue
of the same name. He maintains that he educates people to be
good and, indeed, that he does this apparently by nothing other
than his rhetorical and dialectical art; he leaves aside any and
every specialized knowledge (*Protagoras* 318d). In opposition to
Protagoras's claim, Plato advances the true dialectical art of giving justification, which submits assertions about the good to
question and answer. Plato has a way of making both clear and
convincing that in order to keep oneself from being confounded
in such matters, something else is required besides a technique of
speaking and disputation and besides mere acuity. To be sure,
the ability to differentiate things according to their genera and
thereby expose confusions must be called an art. But more is required than mere acuity to do this.

And true dialectic entails still more. It provides practice in
holding undisconcertedly to what lies before one's eyes as right,
and in not allowing anything to convince one that it is not. Plato
can also call this true dialectic "phronēsis," and with good reason. Here, in the question of the good, there is no body of
knowledge at one's disposal. Nor can one person defer to the authority of another. One has to ask oneself, and in so doing, one
necessarily finds oneself in discussion either with oneself or with

others. For the task is to differentiate one thing from another, to give preference to one thing over another. Later, when Plato characterizes this art of differentiating as *dihairesis* (division), thus making it almost identical with dialectic, he still has in mind less a method than the practical task of differentiating where confusion is especially threatening and prevalent.[8] Such differentiation is not a scientific method in the logical sense. To this extent Aristotle's questioning of the value of dihairesis in demonstration is justified: his objection is that it yields no logically cogent conclusions. One must know ahead of time in which species the thing under consideration falls. And, as a matter of fact, dialectic is not demonstration or proof in the scientific sense of a proof (*apodeixis*), which cogently deduces things from presuppositions. On the contrary, the dialectical art of differentiation presupposes antecedent familiarity with the subject matter and a continuing preview of, and prospect toward, the thing under discussion. Aristotle was right.

But his objection is not a valid objection to Plato. It seems to me that the insight which guides Plato is that such an ability to differentiate dialectically is exactly the same sort of thing as that ability to give justification which characterized the man Socrates in his holding undisconcertedly to what he had recognized to be good. Here we really have knowledge (and not doxa) insofar as someone, knowing his ignorance so well, is completely willing to give justification. After all, Socrates' guiding theme is aretē. In a certain sense aretē is something that one always knows already and always must know already. To use the fashionable word today, aretē requires self-understanding,[9] and Socrates proves to

8. I attempted to make a convincing case for this point at the time that I wrote *Platos dialektische Ethik*.

9. Here again Gadamer has in mind that unity of logos (word, reason) and ergon (deed) that figures so prominently in all his interpretations of Plato: any

his partners that this is what they lack. Plato gives self-understanding a more general meaning: wherever the concern is knowledge that cannot be acquired by any learning, but instead only through examination of oneself and of the knowledge one believes one has, we are dealing with dialectic. Only in dialogue—with oneself or with others—can one get beyond the mere prejudices of prevailing conventions. And only the person who is really guided by such pre-knowledge of the good will be able to hold to it unerringly. Plato has various metaphorical ways of expressing this fact. For example, he says [that such a person can hold to the good] because the good "resides" in him, or because it is "related (*syggenēs*) to him." Thus, unlike the unfortunate victims of Socrates' refutational arts who do not understand themselves, the true dialectician does not allow himself to be artfully misled past the truth. But the converse holds too: whenever someone who knows how to give justification nevertheless goes astray, as Socrates himself occasionally does in Plato's dialogues, he finds his way back and then knows how to articulate what he intended to say better than before. That occurs, for instance, after Protagoras's famous repudiation of a *conversio falsa* which Socrates commits (350c ff.).

---

question about aretē and the good is not merely a question for intellectual inquiry but also an existential question of how I am to understand and lead my life—a question of what I am to do.

One must be careful, however, not to conflate this element of "existential" concern in Gadamer's reading of Plato with the subjectivism of modern existentialism. Neither Plato nor Gadamer begin with the individual subject, but rather with the language we speak and the traditions and customs that constitute our world and from which we as individuals derive. Hence *gnōthi s'auton*, Socrates' "know thyself," really means, know the logoi, our ways of saying things, which lend our world its significances and values. We come to know the logoi and what we are to do not in solitudinous "existing towards death" but in dialogue with others and with ourselves. *Wir sind ein Gespräch*: we are a discussion (cf. *Phaedrus* 230d on Socrates' passion for discussion). TRANSLATOR.

There are places where Socrates with vacuous finesse seems to abandon himself to making formal distinctions, and thereby to disavow his true intentions and to deny that he knows better— for instance, in his first *erōs* (love) speech in the *Phaedrus*. But an inner voice, whether he calls it his *daimonion* or not, will hold him back and compel him to retract what he has said in a second speech. And this retraction is anything but a blind act of submission to a traditional religious rule.[10] Socrates covered his head when he gave the untrue panegyric (*Phaedrus* 257a), and only in the retraction is he once again entirely himself. Only Socrates' retraction places the experience of erōs within the grand and broad setting of Plato's rendering of his master's charisma. Socrates uncovers the true distinctions, as befits one who knows what ought to be known and given justification—as befits, in other words, the dialectician. What the latter is, is expressed mythically in his second speech. There he not only properly identifies the essence of erōs as a god-given gift. Put another way, he not only makes the necessary distinction between "good" and "bad" madness— a distinction that is essential if human beings are to have a true understanding of themselves and what they experience in love. In making this distinction, he shows himself to be a real dialectician, who, in the very process of giving justification, unveils at the same time the nature of dialectic as such. The passion for the beautiful is consumed here in the passion for the true. We will return to this point subsequently.

Thus, in Plato's dialectic the concern is still that Doric harmony of logos (word) and ergon (deed) that gives Socrates' refutational enterprise its particular *ēthos* (character).[11] This har-

10. That is, that one should recant one's blasphemy, in this case, of the god Eros (*Phaedrus* 242e). TRANSLATOR.

11. For a programmatic exposition of the relationship of these two, see my "*Logos* and *Ergon* in Plato's *Lysis*."

mony—or the lack of it in his partners—not only provides the background for Socrates' (often logically unsatisfactory) art of argumentation in the elenchtic dialogues. Even in the so-called dialectical dialogues of Plato's later period it plays a far greater role than is generally acknowledged.[12] For example, one will only be able to understand the *Theaetetus* fully once one has properly evaluated the complete paradox in Theaetetus's giving a sensual-istic answer to the question "What is knowledge?" For Theaete-tus is a brilliant mathematician.[13] Also, the task of differentiating between the philosopher and the sophist, which the *Sophist* dia-logue proposes, can only be carried out successfully by someone who is really (*ontōs*) a philosopher and no mere artist at refuta-tion. From the very start of the *Sophist* the search for the essence of the sophist is guided by the vision of the true essence of the philosopher and dialectician. The Stranger from Elea is no mere artist at refutation, and hence it is quite in the order of things that the essence of the philosopher and dialectician must also be cleared up if one is to arrive at a clear grasp of the sophist.[14] In the *Phaedrus* the task was to distinguish between good and bad madness. Similarly the task here is to distinguish the true dialec-tician from the false one, the sophist. Even here the differentia-

12. Sprague, for example, shows an understanding of the logical fallacy at *Theaetetus* 163 ff. insofar as she quite rightly acknowledges the positive qualities that Plato assigns his Theaetetus figure. However, the pervasive dependence of logos on ergon extends much further into the content of the dialogue than she perceives. See R. Sprague, *Plato's Use of Fallacy* (London, 1962).

13. What Theaetetus is in deed—a mathematician—is a far cry from the po-sition he takes intellectually when he proposes that knowledge is sense percep-tion (*aisthēsis*). TRANSLATOR.

14. Some observations are to be found in my "Plato und Heidegger" (in *Der Idealismus und seine gegenwart, Festschrift für Werner Marx* (Hamburg, 1976, pp. 166–75) concerning the limited success with which the "sophist" can be grasped and the limitations under which, in Plato's view, any comprehension of him is possible at all.

tion by dihairesis is still aimed at differentiating the good from the bad. That this is so becomes fully explicit once again in the *Philebus*, in which the dihairesis is wholly concerned with the good in human life.[15] It makes good sense to call the dialectical virtue "phronēsis."

Let us return from this perspective on things, to which we were led by Plato's use of the word *phronēsis*, to the actual *thema probandum*, namely, that in Plato's eyes knowledge in aretē has something special about it that sets it apart from the technai. On occasion the difference emerges explicitly, for example, in the *Meno* at 74b, where it is declared to be particularly difficult *"mian aretēn labein kata pantōn"* (to take one virtue above all), evidently because conventional morality only knows many different conventional aretai (see 71e ff.). But above all, the difference between aretē and technē is demonstrated by the role that the problem of teaching aretē plays in Plato. The *Protagoras* is of decisive significance in this regard. That aretē can be taught ought to follow as cogently from the character of knowing in aretē as the fact that technē can be taught indisputably follows from knowing in technē. But as a matter of fact, it does not. That is common knowledge, for which Plato can find support as early as in Theognis. In a certain sense the problem at the core of all education is, after all, the fact that unlike the technai, aretē is not teachable. Traditional ethical and moral customs are based not so much on teaching and learning as on taking someone as an example and emulating that example. Xenophon says explicitly that Socrates never promised to be a teacher of aretē, rather that by the example he set—*toi phaneros einai toioutos* (himself appearing to be of such character)—he inspired followers—

---

15. J. Stenzel's "Socrates," in the *Realenzyklopädie der Klassischen Altertumswissenschaften*, vol. 3, col. 856 ff., has already brought this element of *dialegein* (sorting out, selecting) to our attention.

mimoumenoi (emulators) (*Memorabilia* Alpha 2). Ethical norms are passed on with an accepted self-evidentness that social traditions lend them, and Protagoras comports himself quite in keeping with this traditional thinking when he names "all Atheneans" as teachers of political virtue (*Protagoras* 327e). Of course, he leaves unsaid that just these Atheneans can also be teachers of injustice, and Socrates' and Plato's lives are defined in their entirety by precisely this fact that they can. Plato's *Seventh Letter* (325f.) and his interpretation of Socrates' life in the *Apology* fully concur on this: only the demand for justification lays bare the empty presumption in the usual moral and political self-understanding.[16]

But Plato goes even further by contrasting Socrates with the great sophists in his dramas. In this way he shows that precisely by claiming falsely that it teaches by means of a new knowledge, the new ideal of *paideia* secures this conventional morality. For the new ideal of paideia was precisely conscious learning. And just that is what the great sophists of the time, of whom Protagoras is representative, claim they can bring about. They promise that by instructing the student in the new art of speech making and argumentation, they will educate him to be a just citizen of the state—in the ancient sense of taking active part in public affairs. As the *Protagoras* shows, sophistic paideia does not claim at all that, by teaching its art, it is putting new norms in the place of those traditional moral norms whose decisive force is perpetuated through education using paragons of virtue. By its art it claims to impart civic virtue—the same civic virtue as always

16. Compare "Plato's Educational State" and "Plato and the Poets." The problem is that the communal solidarity upon which traditional morality is based has been destroyed. As a consequence, what one uncritically assumes to be right turns out to be nothing more than a rationalization of self-interest (see n. 2 above). TRANSLATOR.

was and always will be—in a new way. Knowledge about aretē
is always sustained and transmitted by all. But the sophist does
what everybody does with "art," and that is what he means
when he praises his new "art" as the perfection of education. We
see this claim equally in Plato's characterizations of both Protagoras and Gorgias. And a lot of what we know of both these men
from other sources—for example, that they were held in high es-
teem by society—accords with Plato's portrayal of them.

But now the Socratic question overturns the whole sophist
claim. Plato shows in the dialogues named for these two sophists—to which group the *Republic*, book 1, the so-called "Thrasymachus," also belongs—what ill fate this paideia's new claim
to be knowledge actually bodes. Theirs is a technical mentality,
which passes itself off as aretē without really being aretē at all.
This pretense is exposed by displaying its radical consequences
in radical immoralists of the cut of a Thrasymachus or a Callicles. In the *Protagoras* the unmasking is not as explicit, but certainly the way is cleared for it. For there is no doubt that there
Protagoras ought to be forced into a radical hedonism as the true
consequence of his concept of knowledge. Precisely by decking
himself out in another garb and thereby evading this radical consequence, he makes clear negatively that it is a conclusion he
would have to draw. In truth, his pragmatic knowledge and his
art are incapable of establishing any other norms or defending
them. Then, in book 6 of the *Republic* (493 ff.), this point is
stated explicitly: the so-called sophists are actually the hirelings
of public opinion. Every one of them teaches nothing other than
the opinions that people form when they get together. And that
is what they call wisdom. The new paideia appears to accom-
modate itself to the traditional system of norms. But this appearance, we see, is false and only obscures the fact that the
traditional concepts of aretē cannot be given sufficient justi-

fication and conceals that this world of norms has itself become equivocal.

Thus the purpose of Socrates' pointing to the paradox in the knowledge of virtue is precisely to show that the traditional world of norms has come to need justification, but that it is incapable of being justified: what this new paideia is really claiming is that it is a technē of success. When it purports to impart a knowledge founded in [what for it is] the self-evident continuing validity of the world of norms, its apparent knowledge proves false, and its sureness of being able to justify itself illusory. As we saw, its pretense is exposed in the *Protagoras* in the caricature of an art of living that would amount to technical knowledge (*metretikē technē*) of how to get the greatest amount of pleasure possible. But most of all, its pretense is exposed in the paradox that all aretē, despite its claim to be knowledge, is unteachable.

One now sees how skillfully Plato's *Protagoras* is composed, and what a powerful statement its dramatic setting makes just by itself. Plato's idea of confronting the famous sophists of the time (Protagoras, Gorgias, Hippias, Thrasymachus) with his Socrates appears to be an invention all his own, and it serves the purpose of defending Socrates against the fateful equation of him with the sophists, an equation that was the reason for his tragic condemnation. Xenophon reports only one other comparable pairing with a sophist—with Hippias (*Memorabilia*, Delta 4)—but it is set up quite differently. The sophist knows Socrates well. He complains that Socrates is forever saying the same things, and that one can never get a positive answer out of him (the theme of the *Clitopho*). Therefore Hippias insists that Scorates himself finally say something positive about to dikaion (what is just). But what Xenophon has Socrates say in response could hardly be based on authentic remembrances. Xenophon's apologetic motif is all too trivial and transparent. Socrates may have argued before the court that he himself never committed an injustice, and Plato also has him say that. However, what Xenophon has Socrates say about to dikaion itself, namely, that it is *to nomimon* (what is lawful), and about the *agraphoi nomoi* (unwritten laws) and in justification of the prohibition of incest and about the gods—all that is colorless. Moreover, Xenophon has the sophist interlocutor agree in the same colorless way in which all the partners in the *Memorabilia* do. The other conversation in Xenophon between Socrates and a sophist (Antiphon) is totally superficial (Alpha 6). In any case, these naively apologetic confrontations bear no similarity to Plato's great sophist dialogues.

In the *Protagoras*, in contrast, Plato displays the falsity of sophistic pseudo-knowledge and of the claim to teach it by confronting this "knowledge" and claim with Socrates' claim to know. And the conclusion with which the dialogue ends says a great deal: Socrates forces the sophist to agree that aretē is knowledge, but for his part he disputes that it can be taught. But if Socrates really took aretē to be knowledge similar in character to the knowledge of technē, he would have to maintain that it *can* be taught. What sort of knowledge, then, is this knowledge that he has in mind that is evidently unteachable? The reader is meant to put this question to himself. In any event, he has to see clearly that the knowledge and justification for it that Socrates seeks has nothing to do with sophistic technē thinking. That it does not is obvious from the start. The doubt about the teachability of aretē dominates the discussion from beginning to end. Even in the opening scene it lurks in the background. Thus the logical point of the comedy-like ending that Plato invents for the *Protagoras* dialogue is most of all this: knowledge in aretē can have the character of neither knowledge in technē nor the knowledge of this new paideia, which boasts of being technē.

The whole series of the Socratic discussions whose conclusions are negative could be advanced to demonstrate the inadequacy of the technē concept for attaining a clear concept of knowledge of the good and of the nature of aretē. The *Meno* is particularly crucial in this regard, for the exposition here is advanced one step further. At first the dialogue deals with the same problem as the *Protagoras*, namely, teachability. And in essence it reiterates the paradox in which the claim that aretē can be given justification gets caught: if it can be given justification, then it can also be taught. Once again, the claim that aretē is knowledge founders on the facts of our moral and political experience. The sons of great men, who have had the best education and upbringing thinkable, are often grave disappointments. Hence something other than knowledge must play the decisive role here, something that Plato calls *theia moira*—divine dispensation.

And now we have arrived at a truly crucial test for the traditional interpretation of Plato. Socrates' own demand that justification be given, which he pursues relentlessly, seems weakened when Plato substitutes "divine dispensation"—the latter appears to provide only half an answer to the problem. Subtle interpreters of Plato see in this divine dispensation an indication that Socrates himself is the only true teacher of aretē. It is certainly correct to say that the end of the failed discussion with Meno points to Socrates as the actual and only teacher. But one has already forfeited the truth of this insight if, at the same time, one misses the general point implied here. Plato's concern is not to sanctify this charismatic Socrates, even if in Plato's eyes he certainly was charismatic. Rather, he is much more concerned with overcoming the false conception of learning and knowing that prevails in the young Meno, as it does in his teacher Gorgias. It is to this end that he adverts to divine dispensation.[17]

The whole discussion with Meno is devoted to this task. One

17. The allusion to divine dispensation at *Republic* 492e is also aimed polemically against sophistic paideia.

need only ask oneself Plato's question: Who was this Socrates and what was his knowledge? After all, he had declared that precisely knowing that one does not know is the real human wisdom. His teaching could never be different from what it always is, namely, demonstrating that his partner does not know, and by doing that, making it urgent that one know and give justification. For someone who has come to seek and question on his own, the pretentious assumptions that Meno, for example, has learned from the likes of Gorgias and advances himself are empty. And emptier still is a sophistry that would argue someone out of seeking and questioning altogether—such a sophistry, that is, as Meno produces with blind acuity. The significance of the *Meno* is that here Plato expressly thematizes the aporia (perplexity) in which the other Socratic dialogues tend to end.

Like these other dialogues, the *Meno* begins with a series of failed attempts to define aretē that disclose sometimes more, sometimes less, clearly that the sole reality behind moral conventions is the pursuit of power. The last answer that Meno ventures virtually says as much. He appropriates the poet's line: *charein te kaloisi kai dynasthai* (to delight in the beautiful and have power) in such a way that *aretē* would mean nothing else but having the power to acquire the beautiful thing that one desires (77b). But Plato takes a new step here. He shows that reaching the aporia in which Meno's attempts to determine the nature of aretē end is the precondition for raising the question of aretē in the first place. But here, raising the question means questioning oneself. The knowledge in question can only be *called forth*. All cognition is re-cognition. And in this sense it is remembrance of something familiar and known.

The conversation with Meno makes this fact clear e contrario. Meno appears on the scene as one who wants to acquire the new wisdom as cheaply as possibly, and he bolts when he is about to be forced to place himself in question. Thus he is just the right foil for allowing us to see what knowing and recognizing actually are. The doctrine of *anamnēsis* (recollection) brings out the true sense of the Socratic question. As one who himself only "reminds," Socrates is a teacher. And in portraying Socrates' deeds, Plato at the same time reminds us that knowledge is recollection, knowing again.

The idea of recollection is introduced here as a myth, which is to say, apparently not as an argument per se but as a sort of religious truth. But one has to view the myth of anamnēsis in the light of the question we are raising. Is it a myth at all? Certainly this doctrine is introduced in the *Meno* like a myth—with references to verses from Pindar and the Pythagorean doctrine of the transmigration of souls. But the authorities upon whom Socrates relies already sound odd. For here we find priests and priestesses who are able to give justification! In the context of Greek religion there is something absurd about that. For Greek religion was not a religion of scripture and orthodoxy but of individual awe and piety and of regular public honoring of the divine. Moreover, the thesis that seeking and learning is recollection is then demonstrated quite soberly with no reference at all to religion. The famous lesson that Socrates gives Meno's slave is far removed from a proof of the religious doctrine of the preexistence of souls. Of course, in every step of this lesson Socrates carefully adheres to the premise that the slave is not taught anything but instead grasps each of the steps himself, the negative ones as well as the positive. In other words, the slave displays a kind of knowledge without ever having "learned" mathematics. But given the lengths to which Socrates goes it is all the more striking that the conclusion drawn at the end is not viewed as validly proved—the conclusion, namely, that there was a time before human beings existed at which the soul already knew things, and that the soul is consequently immortal. On the contrary, any such claim that it has been proved is explicitly retracted (86b). The only thing accepted is the practical certainty that we are better off holding firmly to the belief that one can indeed seek the truth, and that one should not allow oneself to be misled in this search by sophistic objections. And it is accepted *logōi kai ergōi* (in word and deed) (86c). Hence the mythical horizons within which Plato places this certainty—and not without ironic ceremoniousness—serve essentially only to display and explicate the capacity of the human mind to place things in question.

The *Phaedo* demonstrates fully and convincingly that we are not dealing with a religious truth here. There the anamnēsis theme is taken up anew, and once again it is explicated quite unmythologically. The way in which the doctrine of preexistence is "proved" here—by the "prior knowledge" that underlies all knowledge—even has a comical side to it. To be sure, it is made clear here that as religious heritage what this preexistence proof demonstrates with its pseudo-stringency, is worthy of solemn respect. But this comical aspect of the argument makes clear that what is 'proved' hardly lends itself to a rational legitimation in a style such as this. In particular, the sharpening of the argument after Simmias's objection that knowledge could, after all, be given to one at birth makes the discrepancy between the mythical claim and the logical concepts with which the argument proceeds especially palpable. Obviously it is with this discrepancy in mind that Plato has Socrates now venture the following argument (*Phaedo* 76d): since knowledge cannot be attained after birth, it must derive from a "previous" life—unless, that is, it is acquired at the moment of birth. But after all, as the initial ignorance of the newborn shows, it is *not* present at birth. So at one and the same time, it would be acquired and lost—a pretty piece of nonsense, it would appear. And with that Simmias's objection seems to have been disposed of. Or, in the final analysis, is this a hint that we should examine in earnest the concomitance of knowing and not-knowing? For if we do, we might perceive in this concomitance an intrinsic interweaving of cognition and recognition that splits apart into a mythical prior life and a subsequent recollection only in mythological thinking.[18] Whatever the case may be, we must abstract from Plato's mythical mode of presentation if we want to understand what he is getting at. And that requirement holds in regard to the *Meno* as well as the *Phaedo*. Let us, then, attempt to conceptualize some of the things he has in mind.

After he has put the false solutions behind him, the slave in the *Meno* recognizes that a square constructed on the diagonal has the double area he seeks. That he does so implies that he already knows what "double" means—he must know Greek (82b)—and that he keeps his attention focused on doubling and what is double. Accordingly, we have a real seeking here. The slave has enough of an idea of what is sought to recognize that his first at-

18. One of the essential tenets of Gadamer's thought underlies this interpretation, namely, that human beings never have insights that are fully clear and distinct, but only partial insights within persistent obscurity. Thus any *alētheia*, or truth, that they know is embedded in *lēthē*, or forgetfulness. This concomitance of knowing and not-knowing (which Heidegger would call, *Gleichursprünglichkeit*) has far-reaching consequences. For one thing, it renders the project of Cartesian methodology incapable of execution: since there is no certain starting point, no certain conclusions can be drawn. For another, it makes systematic unity and conclusiveness unachievable: we always find ourselves *in media res*— under way in the middle of things whose beginning and end are beyond the horizons of our knowing. Gadamer finds this principle of human finitude throughout Plato and, in particular, in his doctrine of ideal numbers, the one (unit) and the indeterminate two. For Plato, Gadamer maintains, any unitary thing we know is given to us within the indeterminacy that surrounds it. Consequently, our inquiry will remain inconclusive (*unabschliessbar*). See "Plato's Unwritten Dialectic." TRANSLATOR.

tempts to solve the problem by doubling are wrong and to recognize the true solution when it is presented to him. As we know, he does not find it on his own. Socrates has to show it to him (85e). That fact is of no concern, however. The point is that he himself recognizes it as the solution he seeks.

It should be noted that we are dealing with a mathematical insight here, that is, not with a result of empirical generalization. The slave already knows enough of mathematics to accept without question that the problem put to him is eidetic-universal and to grasp it as such without giving it a second thought. The entire path along which the slave is guided to his eidetic insight proceeds through eidetic terrain. Even his first mistaken attempts at solving the problem are meant to be eidetic. They are wrong only mathematically. For him, unlike his master, the insight that his proposals are false is not anything that might cripple him. Instead, it actually makes the right insight possible—an insight that would require only sufficient repetition of the exercise to be stabilized in him as genuine mathematical knowledge (85c ff.).

Here, however, this mathematical example stands for everything that Plato would call real knowledge or insight. One always has *alētheis doxai* (true beliefs) in oneself concerning what ones does not know (*Meno* 85c). Indeed, just this fact emerged in the mathematical lesson: the refutation of false assumptions is needed in order for these to be recognized as false, but that entails that one always already[19] has some idea of what the true as-

---

19. *Immer schon.* This common turn of speech has special importance in Heidegger's work and also in Gadamer's. It underscores the fact that I actually never was, and never will be, in the state of unprejudiced objectivity which the Enlightenment considers prerequisite for valid knowing. Put another way, I am never in an "original position" (Rawls); rather, I can understand what I encounter within my world only because of the pre-knowledge that I "always already" have. Implied here is Heidegger's and Gadamer's theory of the circularity of understanding. Gadamer extends Heidegger's line of thought in arguing for the in-

sumption is. Thus, what is displayed here is the nature of seeking and learning (*zētein, manthanein*) (81d). Seeking and learning presuppose that one knows what one does not know, and to learn that, one must be refuted. Knowing what one does not know is not simply ignorance. It always implies a prior knowledge which guides all one's seeking and questioning. Cognition is always re-cognition.

Plainly that holds especially in regard to aretē. And though the *Meno* too does not say so explicitly either, Meno's renewed evasion of the issue at 86c makes clear even so that the question of what aretē is would necessarily lead us to knowledge of the good (see *Meno* 87 b–d). Knowledge of the good is always with us in our practical life. Whenever we choose one thing in preference to another, we believe ourselves capable of justifying our choice, and hence knowledge of the good is always already involved.

Socrates' recapitulation of the doctrine of anamnēsis in the *Phaedo* is no less instructive. In a masterful analysis he unfolds the argument that shows why all knowing is recollection, and leads us through it step by step. He begins with clear instances of our being reminded of something. A lyre reminds us of a beloved friend. A friend reminds us of his friend. Even the picture of a friend also reminds us of the other friend. And, yes, the picture of a friend also reminds us of the friend himself. We are being led along very artfully here, and the final step is astonishing. In this last case we would not say that we are reminded of the friend, but instead that we recognize him in the picture. Exactly because recognition emerges here as a kind of recollection, or being re-

---

dispensability of tradition and authority for any understanding of our human world. His point is that the "condition of the possibility" (Kant) of my understanding my world is not so much consciousness's interpretive acts or performances as it is consciousness *of* and recollection *of*, what is always already pregiven in the traditional authority of language and customs (*Sitten*). TRANSLATOR.

minded of something, Socrates succeeds in establishing what he set out to demonstrate. In this way recognition is set apart from all learning.

It could be important that this example is not a genuine instance of being reminded. After all, seeing the lyre of his friend does not remind the lover of someone he had forgotten! The friend, in fact, is so close and present that the lover is made to think of him by all sorts of things. It is as if he sees all things— and hence the lyre—in the light of his passion. That is significant. The assimilation of *this* being reminded to being reminded of something forgotten is completely contrived. This fact is made clear negatively by the insertion of *malista mentoi* (better yet) at 73e. In truth, what we have here is far more a matter of *mnēmē* (remembering) than of anamnēsis (recollecting, being reminded of something).[20] And properly speaking, knowing, or cognition, too, is not being reminded of something forgotten. Rather, it is a new revelation about something already known. When I recognize something as something, I view something I know in the light of what I take it to be. I interpret it in regard to something which, for its part, is also known to me and present to mind, "*tēs physeōs hapases syggenos ousēs*" (since the whole of nature of akin) (*Meno* 81d).

We can see that this phenomenon of prior understanding applies above all to our self-understanding in aretē and to the question about the good. After all Meno wanted to evade just this supposition [that we already know the good] and by trying to evade it, he induced Socrates to advance the theory of anamnēsis. But there can be no doubt that even in the *Meno* Plato intends anamnēsis to have a much broader sense which should

20. With regard to the relationships here, compare the extensive excursus in J. Klein, *A Commentary on Plato's* Meno (Chapel Hill, 1965), pp. 108–72. Klein is right in bringing in the *Philebus*.

hold for every sort of real knowing. The dialectical art of making distinctions allows us to distinguish the good from the bad or, as we might say with moral reserve, to distinguish the right thing to do from everything which would not be right. But in its full extent this art has to be applicable to knowing anything worth knowing. In the end, the structure of anamnēsis proves to be co-extensive with all possible questioning. Questioning is seeking, and as such it is governed by what is sought. One can only seek when one knows what one is looking for. Only then, only with what is known in view, can one exclude the irrelevant, narrow the inquiry down, and recognize anything. That is what the *Meno* teaches us.

Another illustration, albeit negative, of what Plato has in mind is the failure of Socrates' sophist interlocutors when they want to do the questioning themselves. The questioner seems to them to play a superior role, to which, accordingly, one should aspire. But questioning is not a technique of role playing. The questioner is always one who simultaneously questions himself. The question is posed for him just as it is for the other person. What we have here is the dialectic of dialogue, and its logical structure is simultaneous *synopsis* (seeing things as together one) and dihairesis (division, or differentiation). Both recognition of what one knows oneself to be—that is, recognition of how one understands oneself—and recognition of everything one knows are always at one and the same time *synoran eis hen eidos* (seeing together as one form) and *kata genē dihairesthai* (separating according to species), which is to say, differentiation. We always find ourselves in dialectical tension with the prejudices which take us in and parade themselves as knowledge but which really mistake the particularity and partiality of a given view for the whole truth. That holds for both the person asked and the person asking. Plato's most abstract way of expressing this phenomenon is to say that we confuse *ta metechonta* (things which take part [in the truth] with *to auto* ([truth] itself) (*Republic* 476d). The beginnings of this idea are to be found in the *Meno*, although it is only later, above all in the *R*·*public*, that we are explicitly compelled to draw this conclusion.

Socrates' statement that aretē is knowledge thus proves to be a provocation. For unlike knowledge, aretē is not teachable, although it cannot be denied that it can and needs to be justified. Now it is obvious that Aristotle openly accepts this positive side of the Socratic paradox of knowledge in virtue. Aretē is not logos (reasoning), says Aristotle, but exists *meta logou* (along with reasoning). I will attempt to make credible that in truth this way of putting things is in complete agreement with what Plato and Socrates intended to say and is implicit in the total "intellectualization" of aretē articulated in Plato's dialogues. The fact that Aristotle—in half agreeing with "Socrates" (*EN* 1144b ff.)—takes the paradoxical equation of virtue and knowledge in Plato and Socrates literally and "corrects" their mistakes, can, in my view, not be advanced as a counterargument. Aristotle has a way of taking statements not as they were intended, but literally, and then demonstrating their one-sidedness. Aristotle's use of dialectic consists in balancing off the one-sidedness of one person's opinion against the one-sidedness of someone else's. And while often doing violence in the process, he thereby succeeds in better articulating his own position and also in conceptualizing previously unquestioned presuppositions. What Aristotle gains from his critique here is the concept of *ēthos* (habituation), which, like every conceptual advance, becomes the source of new questions. These we must raise later under the heading of practical philosophy.

Here, a general hermeneutical insight must be our guide, the clear outlines of which emerge precisely in discussions like the

Socratic ones, but which ultimately applies to any "discussion of the soul with itself" that we call thinking. Statements like "Virtue is knowledge" do not come out of the blue, rather, their sense is determined in part by what they answer or respond to. Socrates is responding to the confusion in the moral tradition, a tradition for which sophism promises the new foundation of a bogus technē, a new "knowledge." Plato and Aristotle seem to have been in complete agreement in their common efforts to fend off this sophistic technical conception of knowledge. In linking logos to ēthos, Aristotle only further formulates what Plato had in mind.

Is not the prevailing view absurd that Plato underestimated the role of habituation and character molding as these are implied in Aristotle's concept of ēthos? After all, Plato fabricates an entire ideal city, the tone of which is set, for all intents and purposes, by a super-ēthos, a formidable habituation in virtue. To be sure, this ēthos component comes to light only in the quasi-mythical exposition of this new super-ēthos and not in conceptual form. The rule of the philosopher-king remains an enormous provocation insofar as it makes it seem that pure knowledge, theōria, is supposed to provide the answer to the human question about the just life, the question of the good. But exactly what, one must ask, is the point of Plato's utopia? Why did he write it? It appears to me that the utopia of the *Republic*, to the extent that it answers the question about the good, aims at the mature conceptual clarification which the *Nicomachean Ethics* offers in its considered analysis of the relationship between ēthos and logos. In any case, Aristotle's ethics itself presupposes the Socratic-Platonic turn to the logos and rests upon the foundation of it.

Therefore it seems justified to me to go ahead with my attempt to get behind the web of polemical-critical relationships that bind Plato and Aristotle together and, for once, to read the moral-philosophic paradoxes of Plato's writings with an eye to what he and Aristotle have in common. The next step in this direction will be an exploration of the relationships between the *Protagoras* and book 4 of the *Republic*.

III

THE *POLIS* AND
KNOWLEDGE OF
THE GOOD

The unity and multiplicity of the so-called cardinal virtues became a problem in the *Protagoras*, and Socrates demonstrated there—albeit often with sophistic means—that these cardinal virtues are reducible to being knowledgeable. As we emphasized above, the sophistry of these means presupposes in principle that Plato is secure in what he is aiming at: the sophistry is there to serve his purposes. Being able to give justification, being responsible for what one does, is essential to the ethical disposition, and that implies that the whole of one's ethical consciousness and ethical being are at stake here. Consequently, giving justification cannot be limited to any single moral phenomenon, tendency to behave, or special skill. Obviously Socrates has this fact in mind when he plays his game of refutational dialectic and juxtaposes particular virtues with the good. In essence, however, his doing so amounts to the same thing as Aristotle's rejection in the *Nicomachean Ethics* of the separation of the aretai from each other and his assignment of the very same unifying function to the logos (rational principle) of phronēsis (*EN* 1144b). The problem figuring in many of Socrates' numerous *elenchoi* (refutations) becomes especially easy to get hold of in the *Protagoras*, insofar as the question concerning the unity of the many virtues is posed there explicitly from the beginning. In particular, the superficiality of conventional moral judgments becomes clear when Protagoras argues for the privileged status of *andreia* (courage) in distinction to the indissoluble unity of the rest of the virtues. Andreia appears to be a special trait required of soldiers. As such, in Aristotle's eyes, it would only be *a physikē aretē* (natural excellence) (1144b and elsewhere). That is exactly what Plato has in mind. In the *Protagoras* Socrates shows that andreia too is knowledge. Plato pursues this line of thought from the *Protagoras* and *Laches* through the *Republic* and into his late work the *Laws*, in which he gives special attention to andreia— in criticism, I think, of just that unyielding partiality to Sparta of which he might well have been accused by readers passing superficial judgment on the *Republic*.

The content of the corresponding book in the *Republic* (4) fully concurs with the Socratic aims of the *Protagoras*. In a certain sense even the theme that provides the framework for the *Republic*, the ideal polis, already gives a preliminary answer to the question raised in the *Protagoras* about the unity of the virtues. That the *politeia* (state) now provides the framework tells us from the start that the issue is unity in multiplicity: the multiplicity of the political classes is ordered to provide unity and concord, as is the multiplicity of the parts of the soul. In book 4 the order of the state is first discerned in *the structure of* its classes, and then the order of the virtues in the soul is discerned in that order of the state. The virtues here are the traditional cardinal virtues. I will call them the *so-called* Platonic virtues because in truth they are not Platonic but traditional. This fact is now generally recognized. One need only closely examine the definitions in book 4 to see that all four of the traditional virtues are artfully stylized in order to emphasize the element of knowledge that they contain. In other words, they are reinterpreted Socratically.

Here, courage—which in the *Protagoras* still provided the point of stiffest resistance to conventional morality—is not only understood as it was there, namely, as knowledge of what is dangerous and what is not. In the *Republic* Plato outdoes this paradoxical and provocative formulation with an even greater paradox. What he really has in mind is thereby made clear: courage is demonstrated not so much in response to fear of an obvious threat as in response to the hidden danger in what is charmingly pleasant (*hēdu*). And in the political realm the latter danger is the danger of flattery, which is more to be feared than the overt threat of an enemy. The universal meaning of courage, to which Plato is pointing, becomes plain if one places courage in a more general and comprehensive frame of reference, one that includes civil courage. Above all, courage is needed in response to the danger of conformism—courage, that is, which does not allow itself to be misled but "knows."

Then, in book 4 of the *Republic*, one can see how in the end all four cardinal virtues very nearly fuse in the knowledge that they all are. This fusion is obviously what Plato wants to display. He wants to show that the old norms, the traditional aretai, having been established on a new basis, have become something different. For now justification of what is good in them is required, and merely choosing a paragon and imitating it no longer suffices. All the aretai are phronēsis. The question that Socrates raises in the *Protagoras* concerning the unity of the aretai—whether they are more like parts of a clump of gold or more like parts of a face—gives us a clear profile of Plato's new understanding of aretē. *Both* comparisons are inappropriate, for both tacitly presuppose a conventional understanding of aretē oriented toward external appearances. Hence both of the alternatives are misleading. Aretē is not to be thought of at all as a unity or multiplicity of ways of behaving primarily presented to an observer. Rather, it is self-knowledge, phronēsis. In the end our behavior attains its unity when our actions are undertaken in regard to the good.[1]

To be sure, Plato's *Republic* confronts us with a difficulty: it introduces the question of knowledge of the good only in a second stage of the argument, as if it were an afterthought. Once the aretai have all been shown to have the character of knowledge, the analogy between the harmony of the classes in the polis and the harmony of the soul—its "health"—would seem to suffice as an answer to the question about the definition of justice. With the conclusion drawn in book 4 the goal has been reached. As is common knowledge, it is only after this apparent conclusion that the question about the megiston mathēma (the greatest insight), the idea of the good, arises, leading us further along winding paths. It is striking that this question about the good does not follow, as one might have expected, from an attempt to

---

1. The thought here can be traced to Kierkegaard too (cf. *WM* 91). In rising above the aesthetic "stage on life's way" to the ethical stage, I move beyond a life that consists in discontinuous "great moments" of aesthetic exhilaration to a life that maintains continuity in temporal transience—to a life, in other words, in which unity and integrity are established within what would otherwise disintegrate in the flow of time. A question worth pursuing would be the extent to which Heidegger's reception of Kierkegaard in *SZ* opened up new possibilities for understanding Plato, say in Gadamer's *PDE*. It is striking that in ethical matters at least, Kierkegaard and Plato emerge in Gadamer's writings as astonishingly close. That by no means says that Plato is an "existentialist" (see ch. 2, n. 9). Of interest to Gadamer is the transition from the aesthetic, to the ethical stage on life's way, not the transition from the ethical to the religious stage, in which the existential decision made in anxiety supersedes dutiful and consistent adherence to what ought to be done (Plato: *to deon*; Gadamer: *das Tunliche*). TRANSLATOR.

establish what the unity is in the multiplicity of the aretai. Nor is the question about the good based on the foundation of that unity when this question is raised in regard to the class of the guardians of the ideal state. And in any case one might find such a foundation for the question of the good missing in what results from book 4, which [merely] defines [the virtues] (435c ff.).

In book 6 (504a) Plato does remind us of the achievement of book 4, the definition of the four virtues—in particular, the definition of dikaiosynē (justice). The insufficiency of the provisional sketch (*hypographē*) (504d) given in book 4 is articulated nicely here by contrasting learning (*manthanonti*) and practicing (*gymnazomenōi*). As early as 503e an omission is also explicitly acknowledged, namely, the failure to say that the guardians must have practice at the various sciences too, so that their "nature" might also be capable of holding fast to the knowledge of what is most important of all—the good. But this line of thought is not really derived from the problems found in aretē. On the contrary, knowledge of the good is simply treated here as something supreme that, as no one would question, is recognized to be indispensable: the crowning accomplishment in the selection and education of the guardians of the ideal state must be knowledge of the good. Thus the connection between founding the unity of aretē in knowledge of the good and the propaedeutic function of the sciences in attaining this knowledge remains more or less obscure.

The education of the guardians, who are to be guided through the various disciplines of the mathematical sciences to dialectic—which is to say, the art of distinguishing—is education by and to theōria (theoretical thinking). This emphasis on theory would appear to lead us far away from the "element of knowledge" contained in every aretē. Indeed, the theoretical concerns in which the guardians are to be educated end up in virtual conflict with the task of political leadership for which the guardians are chosen (*Republic* 519d ff.). Left to themselves, those who have been freed from the cave of murky sense experience and practical routine, those who have been set free for theōria, it could be objected, cannot possibly feel any impetus to return to the cave of politics, in which all knowledge is inexact and where things always go wrong.

Of course Socrates sees no difficulty in defending his position against this objection (*Republic* 519c): in his ideal state there is no private sphere for the individual at all, and hence no question of the happiness of the individual either. Accordingly, he rejects the question of whether those dedicated to theōria would not be done an injustice if they were forced away from the higher fulfillment they find in theōria and, for a time at least, were constrained to pursue the ugly business of politics. Not their own happiness is at issue but the happiness of the whole. Indeed, one even trusts that these ideal guardians of the ideal state will not feel externally coerced but will submit understandingly to the political task assigned to them (520d).

Nonetheless, one must ask oneself if this is really supposed to be an answer to the question of how an existence devoted to theōria sees itself in this world of appearances, the world of social power structures? In Plato's state in the clouds, of course, all problems that would otherwise confuse and distort political and social life are solved ideally. Everyone does what he is supposed to do, and consequently everything is ordered in such a fashion that the whole prospers and flourishes. Just like all the other classes, those who have knowledge and who have been brought up to be leaders of the polis and have been educated in science have careers in the ideal state defined for them in advance, which they must follow. Knowing himself to be almighty, the poet who invents this ideal state is not bothered by the fact that the guardians, who have knowledge and who find their fulfillment in knowing and in dedication to theōria, cannot really be expected to submit docilely to the onmiscient providence of the founder of the state. For Plato each person belongs to the whole.[2]

Thus Plato denies that there is any conflict here. But what does that mean? Does not this very denial prove to the thinking reader that the conflict is real? Indeed it does. To my way of thinking, there appears to be no doubt that Plato has this conflict in mind in all of its sharpness and that he displays it negatively by the very impossibility of his utopian "solution"—the conflict, that is, between knowledge of the truth, to which the theoretical life is dedicated, and actual political life. The choice of an apolitical theoretical life seems fully justified to Plato. The grand excursus in the *Theaetetus* says that it is in plain language, but the point is proven here e contrario insofar as in Plato's ideal city those initiated into theoretical studies must acknowledge the political duty they incur as a condition of their having been selected for such initiation (520a ff.). That they must, fits with Plato's testimony about himself in the *Seventh Letter*. We see there that Plato had recognized that not only in his father city, but in all cities, the entire being of the state was thoroughly and incurably ruined— "unless a reform of quite incredible proportions were to occur"—and that he had turned away from politics completely, *"epainesas tēn alēthinēn philosophian"* (giving himself over to true philosophy) and placing the theoretical search for the truth above everything else. The *Seventh Letter* even makes explicit references to the *ideal* of rule by the philosopher—evidently as negative legitimation for retreating into the private realm.

Still the question is: Does autobiographical interpretation also

2. Keep in mind that the true sōphrosynē is already introduced in book 4 (*Republic* 431e ff.) as aretē common to all.

suffice for understanding Plato's purpose in writing a political utopia and for an exhaustive interpretation of its meaning? This work does indeed constitute a most extreme affront to, and rejection of, Athens. But should we say that it asserts in any way that philosophy and politics are absolutely irreconcilable? Did Plato wish to characterize the conflict between a theoretical and a political existence as irresolvable?

One thing is clear in any event: this ideal state cannot be actualized. All the preconditions for it—from the sharing of women and children to the rule by philosophers to the exodus of all those older than ten years from the city to be reorganized—all these things demonstrate its impossibility. Glaucon hesitates visibly at 484b when he can find no other answer to the question of who would be the right leaders of the polis than "the philosophers." And he remains a hesitant partner to the end: see 541a, *"eiper pote gignoito"* (if it were to come about sometime), and 592a–b, where this is even more pronounced. But what is the whole point of Plato's invention? That we see its absurdity? Is it meant to highlight the impossibility of the ideal? Are we supposed to read this political utopia only negatively and be convinced by it only of the irreconcilability of theoretical and civic life? If so, a great expenditure of intelligence and wit has been wasted. For a blind man would see that such a state is impossible, and precisely its *im*possibility is underscored by the clumsy and circuitous demonstration of its possibility. Does Plato seek nothing more than to show that the conflict between theōria and politics is irresolvable?[3]

On the contrary. Surely one must read the whole book as one grand dialectical myth. On occasion Plato himself virtually says that dialectic is its principle. (See 497e: *"tounantion ē nun"* [the

---

3. Such is the opinion of Leo Strauss and Allan Bloom.

opposite of what is now].) Surely one must take all the institutions and structures in this model city as dialectical metaphors. Of course, reading dialectically does not simply mean taking the opposite of what is said, to be the true belief. Here, reading dialectically means relating these utopian demands in each instance to their opposite, in order to find, somewhere in between, what is really meant—that is, in order to recognize what the circumstances are, and how they could be made better. Per se, the institutions of this model city are not meant to embody ideas for reform. Rather, they should make truly bad conditions and the dangers for the continued existence of a city visible e contrario. For example, the total elimination of the family is intended to display the ruinous role of family politics, nepotism, and the idea of dynastic power in the so-called democracy of Athens at that time (and not only there).

Indubitably, one must read the argument for the rule of philosophers just as dialectically as everything else that is said about this splendid state in the clouds. This argument is not meant to specify a way to actualize the ideal city. But it is not intended either solely as a negative demonstration of its impossibility. Rather it uncovers something—and not only the obvious fact that no polis would let itself be governed by such philosophers. Is the paradox of the philosopher-king not also meant to give us the positive insight that both aiming at the good and knowing reality pertain to the political actions of the true statesman as well as to the true theoretical life? In support of this thesis one could appeal to biographical facts—I mean Plato's repeated attempts with Dionysius II in Syracuse. Plato certainly had no intention of proposing communal women and children to this tyrant, nor later to his friend Dion, to whom he made very reasonable recommendations—for instance, that of a general amnesty. But the same point could be deduced directly from what Plato says using this utopia. Making the ideal city possible in reality is of so little concern to him that even the question of whether one should make the philosophers rulers or educate the rulers to be philosophers can be left open.

The sole issue is what the paradox of the philosopher-ruler means, that is, what it uncovers about rulers and ruling generally. On the one side, we have the law inherent in all power, according to which power never aims at anything but the increase of itself. On the other side, in opposition to this law, we have the individual who gives himself fully to knowledge and for whom power is of no interest. He knows something better, something higher, to which he wishes to devote himself. When Plato opines that such a person is more suited than anyone else to direct public affairs, he thereby exposes what seductiveness there is in having power: power wants only itself. The education of the guardians has the purpose of making them immune to this seduction. The point "in between" to which Plato directs us here is a state so arranged that the exercise of the power of government will be carried out as a public office and not exploited as a chance to advance one's own interests. My contention is that there is more significance here than the merely negative insight into the incompatibility of philosophy and politics. And it is right when one sees the institution of modern professional officialdom and the ideal of honesty in public officials [foreshadowed] in Plato's requirement [of immunity to the seductiveness of power].[4]

That we are meant to read this projection of an ideal city dialectically is confirmed most of all by the way in which Socrates paints in the transition from this ideal construct to historical reality with its cycle of constitutions—the famous miscal-

4. Cf. Hegel on the principle of modern states: "Thus essentially Plato's requirement is met here" (*Sämtliche Werke*, ed. Glockner [Stuttgart, 1927], vol. 14, p. 195).

culation of the marriage number (546d). The mystifying, yet ingenious, thing about this invention of Plato's, it seems to me, lies
in the fact that this comical shortcoming of a comical institution
symbolically displays why no system of human social order,
however wisely planned or thought out, can endure. What can
only be brought about by an artfully contrived institution will in
the end be done in by its own artificiality. This is the insight
Plato gives us here. The successful calculation of mating, which
insures the continuance of the ideally ordered polis, fails not because of malevolence or external forces, but because of its own
complexity. That is a true statement concerning something we
all know to be the reality of any humanly planned economy: be
the rationality of the planning ever so highly developed, in the
execution of it there is always the power of coincidence, and
above all, there is always human shortcoming. Because we are
human beings, not because we planned mistakenly, even an ideal
self-sustaining organization in full accord with the plan for it
will nevertheless go under in the rolling seas of historical life. To
say this is not at all to deny the task of reason to shape action
reasonably. Book 8 of the *Republic* undertakes to show that wisdom and reason are not only at home in the game of utopianism,
but that in our dealings with "real" historical life too, foresight
and insight are attainable within certain limits. The doctrine of
the cycle of state constitutions presented in book 9—this brilliant example of intellectual penetration of the course of history—confirms that human reason is not restricted to the realm
of utopia and strict ideal order. On the contrary, it is fully capable of expanding into the historical world of vague regularities.
The disorder of human things is never complete chaos. Ultimately this disorder represents the periphery of a sensibly ordered universe that under any circumstances would have its periphery. That *there is order, albeit finite in human events* is

brought out above all by the fact that in Plato's dialogical fiction the *Timaeus* follows the *Republic*. To display the republic that is really supposed to come into being, the entire grand project of the demiurge's ordering of the world, which the *Timaeus* portrays, is necessary.[5]

The question that guides our inquiry here is how Plato unites his concern with the Socratic question about aretē and the good with his scientific program. If we are to find an answer to it, the requirement that we read dialectically must also be taken to heart in regard to the assertions in the *Republic* concerning scientific knowing.[6] In respect to interpreting the allegory of the cave, reading dialectically entails that we abandon all attempts at an exact interpretation of this wonderful and many-layered metaphor regarding its bearing on the theory of scientific knowing. Instead, we must focus on only one point, namely, what function the allegory has within the course of the discussion. Here there is no ambiguity: it is intended to dispel the illusion that dedication to philosophy and the theoretical life is wholly irreconcilable with the demands of political practice in society and the state. The theme is the blinding by the brightness that befalls

5. The demiurge, it will be noted, is always confronted with intractable *anangē* (necessity). Hence he can create order, but never complete order. "Demythologized," what we have here is the principle of unity or order within indeterminancy, the one and the indeterminate two (see ch. 1, n. 22). TRANSLATOR.

6. The German appears here in adjectival form: *wissenschaftstheoretisch*. *Wissenschaftstheorie* (translated here as "theory of scientific knowing") is the theory of science in a broad sense of science that would include not only the natural, but the social and human, sciences, which is to say, any body of knowledge. One of its major concerns is methodology. Of particular importance in this work will be the method appropriate to the "science" of practical philosophy, and how it differs from method in epistēmē and technē respectively. Gadamer maintains that Plato and Aristotle are alike in arguing that the method of practical philosophy must be rigorously distinguished from any sophistic "technical" method. TRANSLATOR.

those accustomed to the dark, and conversely, the blinding of those who leave the brightness and enter the dark. The allegory is supposed to explain why those caught up in the practical life consider the theoretical life worthless (515d and 515e). The story is intended to enlighten us regarding this putative worthlessness of the theoretical human being in practice. One must not only get used to the light; one must also get used to the dark. Those who return from the light of the true day to the twilight of the cave are also blinded at first by the contrast in brightness. That they are does not imply that they are really blinded or are incapable of getting oriented there. Plato tells us that their blindness passes quickly (517a).

Evidently a common objection made to Plato was that philosophy makes one unfit for real life. Plato's desire to defend philosophy against this criticism completely dominates the *Gorgias* (see 485a), and this motif is often heard elsewhere in Plato. It was generally believed that philosophy had a place only in the years of youth, and that it ought not to be continued for long: one must seek entry into political life early enough and give up philosophy. In the *Republic* Adeimantus appoints himself the advocate of this general view (476d). In response, Plato's program for education of the guardians, which lasts decades, develops the idea of the absolute primacy of the theoretical life. Only unwillingly, and only for a limited time, he says, would someone consent to interrupting this life by taking a political office.

One must perceive the deliberate provocation in what Plato is saying when he expressly proposes that after ten years have already been devoted to the study of the sciences, twice as much time then be spent on the exercise of dialectic as on gymnastics. At thirty years of age, the future guardians are to be schooled in dialectic for five years. Then they should assume subordinate political offices for fifteen years. Only when they are fifty are they considered mature enough for the task of political leadership—a task at which they would take turns for a relatively short time. They should continue to spend the larger portion of their time in dedication to a life of study.

It is from this perspective that we must understand the ascent from the cave to the true day and the vision of the true sun. Herein lies its dialectical function within the context of the discussion. And in comparison, interest in the relevance of the allegory to a theory of scientific knowing remains entirely in the background for the time being. Even the fundamental distinction in Plato between doxa (belief) and epistēmē (science, knowledge) (476b ff.) is not introduced at first in the context of epistemological theory. Rather, within the framework of the *Republic*, its function is to prepare us for the paradox of the philosopher-king.

The way in which the allegory of the cave is introduced also leaves the epistemological aspect of the subject matter in the background for the time being. At first it seems that the knowledge to be preferred to all other knowledge is knowledge of the good in the practical, political realm, and this alone is taken to be the knowledge characteristic of those emancipated individuals called to be leaders—knowledge, that is, *tou dikaiou* (of the just) (517d) and *kalōn te kai dikaiōn kai agathōn peri* (concerning things beautiful, just, and good) (520c).

To be sure, it becomes clear subsequently that the way traversed in getting used to the light that the allegory describes—a way which begins with shadows, passes on to reflections, images, and nocturnal stars, and then ends with the sun—is a way to the sciences, through the sciences, and beyond them. Nonetheless, nothing is said either here or later about the application of such theory to human practice. The allegory deals exclusively with the superiority of those who know the good over those who remain caught in moral, political conventions. This fact is displayed particularly well when, in first introducing the paradox of the philosopher-king, Plato places him alongside the eroticist, who loves everything beautiful, and the spectacle-seeker. All three are alike in the universality of their passion. Glaucon is so little mindful of the sciences when the philosopher is spoken of that he even interchanges the spectacle-seeker's curiosity with thirst for knowledge (475d). That conflation, of course, is seriously misleading. Whoever is drawn to spectacles, whoever is swayed back and forth in indiscriminate curiosity about everything there is to see, has in truth no similarity whatever to the philosopher. Indiscriminate passion for novelty constitutes the extreme opposite of philosophy, for philosophy has to do with the just and the unjust, the good and the bad, or, as Plato puts it, with discriminating between the beautiful and the ugly.

To be sure, in what follows it is shown that such a sense for *the* just, *the* good, and so forth, implies a fundamental distinction between what is known and what is believed—the distinction, namely, between the "one beautiful thing" itself and everything which only participates in it (*ta metechonta*). To this extent, that sense of the just and the good is indeed philosophy, which is to say, that it passes beyond the question of the conventional "just and good." This notwithstanding, the allegory of the cave is, as we saw, applied to nothing other than the life of the polis. It is stated expressly that those who have returned will have to deal with the shadows and images of the dikaion, which is to say, with what Plato calls *ta tōn anthrōpōn* (human things) (517c) or *ta anthrōpeia* (that which is of human concern) (517d). Accordingly, one ought not to take the description of the cave and the superior insight of those who have been led upward to the true sun to imply that those who have thus been liberated are, by virtue of their comprehensive knowledge of all true things, better prepared for the upcoming competition—more experienced, more provident. That is not the point here. On the contrary, the cave-dweller knows full well how things tend to go in social and political life and what practices promise to be successful there. What he does not know and what he does not even ask about is the good, for the sake of which all these practices are to be carried out.

Hence the contrast between theoretical knowledge and political practice that is portrayed here—so that it might ultimately be transcended—is not the contrast between theory and practice in the modern sense. What we mean when we oppose theory to practice in our language usage today has to do entirely with the realm that Aristotle calls technē and nothing to do with what is under consideration in Plato's projection of a state—nothing to do, that is, with the ideal of theōria and its relationship to political reality. But just like Aristotle, Plato, of course, knows full well the problem of theory and practice in the realm of technē, which is to say, on the one hand, in any realm in which the concern is to apply general rules, but, on the other, in the realm of general experience having to do with the relationship between ends and means in practical or political action. Here we are dealing with a knowledge of rules, knowledge which, per se, contains nothing to ensure that it is applied correctly. Hence, as is well known, Aristotle rightly observes that the practitioner, for example, the healer, can be more successful than the specialist, for example, the scientifically educated doctor (*Metaphysics*, Alpha, 981a12 ff.). Plato is no less aware of this fact. He explicitly acknowledges the importance of practical experience in his program of education (*Republic* 484d, 538e), and more generally, he sees the hermeneutical problem which is entailed in every use of rules, that is, in their correct application.

One need only compare the thorough discussion of this prob-

lem in the *Phaedrus* (268 ff.). There—with an eye to the knowledge of rules in rhetoric—medicine and the arts of writing
drama and composing music are cited, in all of which there is
also "general" knowledge. That a natural ability remains indispensable is not disputed (269d), but besides having that ability,
education in the art is necessary. Moreover, as the *Phaedrus*
shows by means of Socrates' ironic dissimulation, in the case of
the art of oratory that means that the true art presupposes both
dialectical knowledge of the subject matter and dialectical
knowledge of "souls." Only he who has this double knowledge
is a true rhetorician. Here Plato specifically adds that the rhetorician must also be able to apply all this knowledge correctly in
practice: *"dei dē tauta hikanōs noēsanta meta tauta theōmenon
auta en tais praxesin onta te kai prattonmena"* (it is necessary
that once he knows these things sufficiently, he see them actualized in practice and being done) (271e). Clearly this necessity
pertains to every technē. Moreover, it would seem to me that the
art of measuring what is "fitting," spoken of in the *Statesman*,
also accords with this argument. We shall return to this point
later.

In any case, this hermeneutical problem of concretizing [a general rule] has no bearing on the relationship between politics and
philosophy or on the tension between the political and the theoretical ideals of life. Certainly, application of a technē always
presupposes practice and experience. But the procedure remains
one and the same, whether it be the practice of the educated specialist who knows the reasons for the practical measures he takes
or only the action of an experienced man. On the other hand,
when Plato expatiates in his allegory on the relationship between
the political practitioner and the person who returns to the cave,
his concern is to draw a distinction of a very different sort.
Whether the political practitioner in this or that field is at the

same time an experienced specialist, for example, a military strategist, seaman, or the like, has no bearing at all on the issue at stake. The good that the one who returns to the cave has seen outside is nothing that those chained in the cave want to know anything about.

Their obliviousness can be stated in simple terms. Plato himself alludes to the fact that the art of the navigator per se does not insure that the work he has done well will lead to the good. Agamemnon's navigator might well have had doubts whether he had done something good for his master by bringing the voyage to a safe conclusion (*Republic* 601ff.). In technē the process of production is subordinated to utility, and this subordination sets a limit to technē which, as Aristotle points out (*EN* Zeta 4), excludes it from making any claim to be an aretē.

The way in which Plato organized the ideal city in book 4 already made clear that real knowledge, which one could also call *sophia* (wisdom), is distinct from specialized knowledge of any subject matter (428b ff.). In book 4 this specialized knowledge is depicted in such a way that the city as a whole could be "well advised" (*euboulos*) by it, and likewise the soul: *"echōnti tēn hyper hapasēs tēs psychēs promētheian"* (it has care of the entire soul) (441e). Here the good is still circumscribed simply as knowledge of what is advantageous (*sympheron*) for everyone and for the whole. It can scarcely be overlooked that here in book 4 the word *agathon* is avoided.[7]

---

7. Plato's reservation of the actual question about the good for book 6 would seem to be fundamental to the composition of the *Republic* as a whole. Whether a four-book *Republic* ever existed or not, the effortless and fortuitous introduction of the question of the sharing of women and children, which leads to the extended discussion, may surely be assumed to be as deliberate as the avoidance of the word *agathon* in book 4.

That it is accords quite well with the fact that in book 6 Plato sets the question of knowledge about the good in total opposition to a life led in doxa, that is, in mere conventions, and that to this end he even places knowledge of the good in analogy to knowledge of one's own advantage (505d). There we read that as far as the just and the beautiful are concerned, many might content themselves with an appearance, with what is currently accepted, *ta dokounta*. With regard to the good, on the other hand—and that means even with regard to the benefit that one hopes to have from something—the consensus of others is of no importance to an individual. Only the real advantage counts (*ta onta*). It is instructive that here the rationality in the relationship of means to ends suffices to illustrate the knowledge involved in knowing the good—suffices, that is, to establish irrefragably that it transcends all conventions. Nobody contents himself with merely conventional concepts when the issue is the utility of the means to be chosen.

Now one could also view the so-called technai (the knowledge of the handworker and the so-called sciences) in the same way, that is, as knowledge of the right means, and hence as knowledge of a relative good. Evidently that was the reason why technē knowledge was paradigmatic from early on for the Socratic art of persuasion. But this knowledge is not the knowledge that is of ultimate importance to human beings as human beings, for it fails to provide an ultimate justification. In other words, it knows nothing of "the good itself."

Plato has various names for the knowledge of the good, knowledge which by giving justification sets itself apart from all technai and epistēmai (sciences). For example, he speaks of it as a *dynamis tou dialegesthai* (ability to distinguish dialectically) (532d), a *methodos* (method), and an epistēmē (333c). In so doing, he orders it among these modes of knowing and opens the way for the misunderstanding that knowledge of the good is a highest, teachable knowledge that is to be attained at the end of a long course of education leading through all the mathematical disciplines. Here the bond between knowledge and action seems to tear apart completely—the bond, that is, between those two things which, in the Socratic question, were so closely connected that aretē itself appeared to be knowledge. But what is the significance of "good" in the mathematical sciences? To be sure, in the discussion of different disciplines, its usefulness for the handwork of war is mentioned repeatedly. But here Socrates is all too obviously responding to the trivial expectations that his partners have in regard to any knowledge in the service of the polis. It is for Glaucon's sake when Socrates says that one must take care that such education is not useless for warriors (511d), or when, in appending a sequel to his program of education, he starts with numbers and arithmetic and points out himself their indispensability for the technē of waging war. It becomes clear, nevertheless, that this reference to war and warriors does in fact make some sort of sense within [the discussion concerning] the education of the guardians of the ideal city when Plato refers back to a fundamental line of argument for him first stated in book 2: the close connection between self-control and having power. He first opened up the political dimension as such with that theme, and I have elaborated on this connection in my "Plato and the Poets." At this point in the dialogue, however, this connection is no longer the issue. Hence, when it is said in the summary at the beginning of book 7, for instance, that guardians trained in dialectic are "the best in philosophy just as they are the best suited for war" (543a, and similarly 525b), "best" is always meant in the conventional sense and has an almost ironic overtone. The issue is actually something else. From the beginning, Socrates proclaims his program to be an entirely new kind of education (518b), in which the concern is not so much with learning something as with turning "the whole soul" around (521c). For instance, when Glaucon emphasizes in regard to astronomy that it is useful for the art of waging war, Socrates takes Glaucon's argument as an occasion to criticize his worry about the masses of people to whom the sciences could appear useless (527d). As a matter of fact, in what follows Plato is emphatic in always justifying exercises in the mathematical sciences by their single essential preparatory function: they ready us for knowledge of the idea of the good. (Plato says this explicitly at 526e.) Particularly in respect to music and astronomy, this preparatory function entails a turn quite unexpected by Socrates' partners, the turn, namely, away from the audible and visible to the purely mathematical-arithmological. It is difficult to see how this turn is still supposed to bear on the Socratic question [about aretē] and on the precondition for asking it—knowledge of one's own ignorance.

Then, in a concluding summary, it is asserted that the preparatory curriculum through the mathematical disciplines is designed to lead what is best in the soul (*to beltiston en psychei*) to a vision of what is best in reality (*pros ten tou aristou en tois ousi thean*) (532c). This assertion, made with recourse once again to the myth of the cave, also readies us for the final transition to dialectic, and it is said of dialectic here, in similar fashion, that it pulls the soul up out of the mire (533d). But just what this assertion is supposed to mean is so obscure for [anyone schooled in] the ways of thinking prevailing at the time that Glaucon calls it "difficult." He would like to be instructed in the skill of dialectic in the way one is instructed in a new science having its special objects and methods. This expectation scarcely speaks for his understanding of the matter. And indeed such expectations in regard to Plato's thought are never fulfilled. In the realm of dialectic, there is no differentiation that would correspond to differentiation in the mathematical sciences.

Thus this curriculum of education, insofar as it leads through the sciences up to dialectical knowledge of the good, leaves us with a peculiarly ambiguous result. The deduction and summary with which the previous arguments conclude would appear to be the crowning piece in the theoretical ascent to dialectic. Yet, in fact, they are more than that. The issue is now the good itself, which would correspond to the sun in the allegory, and now the question of what this is, is finally supposed to be answered without a metaphor (*oud' eikona*) (533a). It turns out, however, that this particular question literally dissipates in the universality of [inquiry concerning] everything that truly is: the dialectician is characterized as one who strives to find what any and every existent reality truly is (*auto ge hekastou peri ho estin hekaston*) (533b), one who grasps the logos (concept, definition) of being of each thing (*ton logon hekaston lambanonta tēs ousias*) (534b). This characterization is given in order to distinguish dialectic from the mathematical sciences, which are to be termed mere *dianoia* (understanding), and in this regard it is entirely accurate.

But then the good too is said to be an object—supposedly in "just the same way" (*hōsautōs*) [as the other realities]: like the *ousia hekastou* (being of each), one must separate the idea tou agathou (idea of the good) from everything else, and, as if in battle, one must endure tests of mettle and make one's way undistractedly through every challenge *aptōti tōi logōi* (with a logic that cannot be overthrown). If not, one will recognize neither the good itself nor anything else which is good.

We must pause here. This "in just the same way" is a source of no small difficulty. Certainly one can comprehend that in the case of the good too, it is the procedure of the dialectician—giving justification—that alone can prevent our being confused by false similarities, being guided by mere conventions, or being seduced by flattery. In the imagery of the *Republic*, book 2, the dialectician is like a "philosophical dog" [in his faithfulness to his task]. But it is astonishing even so that the idea of the good appears here merely ordered alongside the other ideas. This equation suggests that it is just one idea among others. At the very most, one could say only that the dialectical differentiation of this idea from all others is especially difficult to carry out because of the particularly strong interference of interests and preferences in this case. And perhaps one is also supposed to detect, if one listens carefully, that cognition of the good, which is either to be won or lost here, is more important than anything else for one's whole life. That it is, is brought out negatively by the juxtaposition of "life here" with Hades (534c).[8] But no retraction of the likening of the good to the other ideas is implied thereby. To say that one can only know everything else good if one knows the idea of the good is to say practically nothing, for this way of putting things holds just as much for all the other ideas also. At the beginning, too, the question about the good was introduced with the same schematic formula—namely, that it is the thing by virtue of which everything else (*kai dikaia kai talla* [what is

8. "And it is the same in regard to the good: if someone is unable to define the idea of the good by giving a reasonable account of it, abstracting it from all else, and fails to get through to it, getting through all tests and seeking to defend it against all these with a logic not to be overthrown (*aptōti tōi logōi*), as if in battle—if all this be true of him, you would not say that he has recognized either the good itself or any other good. Rather, you would say that if he has attained to any image of it at all, he has done so through opinion and not through science, and that in dreaming and slumbering this life away, he will land in Hades before ever awakening here and sink into the deepest sleep" (*Republic* 534c). (Text provided by translator.)

just as well as everything else]) becomes useful and good (503a). But how are we to reconcile the manifold of true reality with the unity of the true good? And at the expense of what? Should the reality that is split apart into the multiplicity of ideas be sacrificed, so that, by suspending all "hypotheses" of ideas (*tas hypotheseis anhairousa*) (533e), one ascends to a good that would no longer be the good of each particular (*hekastou*)? Or should the "separate" (*aphelōn*) good be sacrificed, so that the good would then be in everything good, and so that, like all ideas, it would have its true being only in what participates in it? The text here calls for no such radical interpretation. Since we are faced with an explicit "in just the same way," we cannot treat the matter as if we were dealing with some new, ultimate step leading from the multiplicity of ideas to the "principle" of the one and the good. On the other hand, one would certainly not want to say that the idea of the good is comprehended "in just the same way" as all the other ideas. Is the idea of the good only one of the ideas? And if so, what happens then to the "one, [and] good"?

Hence we must ask ourselves: In the end, is it only Plato's mythical way of speaking that involves us in this apparent dilemma? Can one develop from Plato's metaphor a better way of putting the question? Let us reexamine the metaphor and our interpretation of it. Back when Plato introduced the analogy between the sun and the idea of the good, things looked quite different. There, the good was not *ousia* but was explicitly said to be "beyond" ousia, exceeding it in majesty and power (509b). There, we found no "in just the same way," but instead a surprising new step. And it would still be a new step even if it were to signify only a new insight into what can be called "true," what thereby constitutes the being of any given thing.

For, initially, one can interpret the comparison of the good with the sun at 508e in the following way: what gives alētheia (truth) to what is known and gives the capacity to know it to the one who knows it is supposed to be the idea of the good—just as visible things are visible and the eye can see, thanks to the sun that sheds light. Thus, to begin with, the idea of the good is the cause of knowledge and of truth (epistēmēs or *gnōseōs*, and alētheias). Obviously the point is the analogy with seeing and the visible, and their dependence on light. Just as seeing and light are sunlike, so too, knowing and truth are to be called "good-like," even if they do not yet count as the good itself, that is, as *tou agathou hexis*: the character the good has about it, what it is. And to this extent the analogy is indeed most expressive. One can completely set aside the question of the cause of the light, the question, that is, about the sun. True being—the *noumena* (objects of intellection), the *ontōs onta* (things that really are), the eidē (forms)—appears in thinking in the same way that light connects the visible with seeing: the good makes thinking what it is. The capacity (*dynamis*) for something is, after all, always defined by what it is a capacity for, and by what it effects (*eph' hoite esti kai ho apergazetai*) (477d). Thus, what lights up (*katalampei*) as *alētheia te kai to on* (truth and being) (508d) allows thinking to be thinking, that is, allows it to *noun echein* (have reason, be right, *avoir raison*) in that nice double sense of both getting an insight and being capable of reasoning. With this formulation it seems clear that the whole realm of the *noēta* (things thought of) has been opened up.

   The metaphor of light accomplishes all this, and it is significant that in the scene in the *Parmenides* in which the young Socrates is supposed to clarify the participation of the many particulars in the idea, he takes refuge in the same marvelous metaphor. *Plato's own recourse to the metaphor of light is plainly behind Socrates' answer in the *Parmenides* that the idea is like the day. Socrates wants to say that just as things are only visible in the one light of day that floods around them, so too the idea is visible only to the extent that it emerges in thinking. This means, however, that the idea is only visible to the extent that it allows the beings which appear to be thought of as *what* they are. Thus we have a threefold methexis (participation) here: (1) the methexis of the individual in the idea, (2) the methexis of the soul in the idea, but ultimately, (3) the methexis of the ideas in each other—for any thinking of something is both a delimiting-from and a combining-with (cf. the *Sophist* on dihairesis and *synagōgē*). My thesis, then, is this: these three kinds of methexis are nothing but aspects of one and the same relationship. To think of "this here" as "what" it is, is always at the same time to differentiate the "what" from the "this." But to differentiate the "what" is always to differentiate one "what" from another "what": the impurity in the appearing "this" is in truth the existence of some other pure thing in it.[9] This circumstance provides the background for the dialectic in the *Parmenides*.*

There, of course, Socrates shows himself incapable of keeping a firm hold on the sense of the metaphor of light and of elevating it to the conceptual level. He is still young. In truth, Aristotle is the first who could. He did so in availing himself of the distinction between *poiein* (doing or making something) and *paschein* (suffering something), or *poiētikon* (active) and *pathētikon* (passive), to conceptualize the structure of nous (intellect). In Aristotle too, nous enables, "makes" (*poiei*), thinking, *hōs hexis tis* (as a kind of condition), just as light *"makes potential colors

9. The impurity of fire, for instance, is coals or ashes, which to someone who might use them for fertilizer are something else pure. It is not by accident, Gadamer points out, that one says *reiner Schmutz*—pure filth. Thus there are indeed ideas for "mud" and "hair" though Socrates is reluctant to admit it. TRANSLATOR.

into actual colors"* (*De anima* 430a14 ff.).[10] The principle of
the good, then, would seem to have the function of a principle
only in epistemological matters.

But if we follow Plato's text, we see that Socrates takes a decisive step beyond this interpretation of the allegory. And when he
does, the special status of the idea of the good again becomes a
problem. For now the "transcendence" of the good emerges with
all its ontological implications. And not without a dramatic
mise-en-scène: as the sun bestows upon things not only visibility
but also their coming into existence, their growth, and their nur-
ture, without it itself being "becoming" (*genesis*), so too the idea
of the good, without having "being" itself, is said to give being,
to einai kai tēn ousian (being and reality) (509b), to what is
known in thinking. The comparison forces us to take this ascent
beyond being in such a way that the good becomes the "cause"
of the being of the many ideas. But of course the question remains: "cause" in what sense? The word "cause" (*aitia*), which
we know as the fourth genus of the *Philebus*, is not used here—
either for the sun or for the idea of the good. On the contrary,
the text moves in the semantic field of *dynamis* (power): *pare-
chein* (allowing), *pareinai* (standing by), *proseinai* (being present). The rendering of the good that Socrates gives (511b) makes
unequivocally clear that here the good is interpreted as *tou*

---

10. "But since, as in the whole of nature, to something which serves as matter
for each kind (and this is potentially [*dynamei*] all the members of the kind) there
corresponds something else which is the cause or agent (*poiētikon*) because it
makes (*poien*) them all, the two being related to one another as art to its material,
of necessity these differences must be found also in the soul. And to the one [pas-
sive part of] intellect, which answers to this description because it becomes all
things, corresponds the other [active part of intellect] because it makes all things
(*panta poien*), like a sort of definite quality (*hōs hexis tis*) such as light. For in a
manner light, too, converts (*poiei*) colours which are potential into actual 'colours'" (*De Anima* 430a10–16; translated by R. D. Hicks).

pantos archē, the "starting point (principle) of everything." Consequently—and just as unequivocally—it is the good from which the descent begins and from which the multiplicity of the ideas that make up the noetic realm originates. It is explicitly stated in regard to the mathematical-dianoetic realm (511d) that the multiple ideas are called noetic because they exist *meta archēs* (by virtue of the starting point), which is to say, because they derive their intelligibility from the archē. There would be no problem here in saying that this mathematical realm of *entia rationis* derives not only its intelligibility but also its being from the archē. The interrelationships here in the dianoetical realm of the mathematical, at least, have been splendidly explained in the investigations of Konrad Gaiser.[11]

Now the realm of dialectic, of course, is first reached when we pass beyond the dianoetical, and only then have we taken the full measure of what truly is: *"autou ge hekastou peri ho hekaston"* (concerning each thing itself, what it is in itself) (533b). Hence we can say that wherever we imprint the seal "it is"—wherever, in other words, we make use of words and speech and say sentences—we dream about being (*oneirōttousi men peri to on*) (ibid.). But for the time being we just dream. Only the dialectician awakens from the hold that the dream of the life-world has on us. And "waking up" is precisely what he does: he suspends the hypotheses in which our linguistic interpretation of the world is set down, and in thought alone, he inquires what lies behind them.[12]

---

11. K. Gaiser, *Platos ungeschriebene Lehre* (Stuttgart, 1963).

12. It is here that Plato moves beyond our world of things as they are originally given to a "metaphysical" world (Heidegger). What Gadamer emphasizes is that this transition occurs primarily within Plato's approach to *language*. Given the ambivalences of language as it is ordinarily spoken, it is all too susceptible to sophistic manipulation. Consequently, Plato finds himself forced to seek secure

It is common knowledge that Plato discusses the hypothesis of the eidos in the *Phaedo*. The hypothesis of the eidos, it is argued there, should not be involved in dialectical dispute prematurely, that is, without prior testing and scrutiny. In the *Phaedo*, however, it also remains uncontested that when all is said and done dialectic must be given a final justification. In his quest for an ultimate starting point for that justification, the dialectician suspends, one after another, the hypotheses set down in our discourse. And the same thing holds here in the *Republic*. Thus, in both the *Phaedo* and the *Republic* we are led by dialectic up to the archē that is the one. And just as Aristotle did, we may discover in this one the duality of one and two. But there are reasons for assuming that this first thing, or principle, does not serve as the foundation for a system of ideas that could be deduced from it. Apart from the paradigmatic case of the sequential mathematical disciplines, the concern is always with limited realms wrested from the apeiron (indefinite), within which the dialectician attains his insight.

In the *Philebus* Socrates gives the examples of musical tones and of letters and phonemes. These, certainly, are examples of the one's unfolding itself into the many. For letters, like phonemes, have systematic character: "*oud an hen auto kath' hauto*

---

univocal ideas behind our ordinary "linguistic interpretation of the world." Gadamer finds here the beginnings of formal logic as we know it today, that is, the ideal of a univocal sign system that would allow us to transcend the confusions induced by the unclarity of ordinary language (cf. *WM* 383 ff.). Still, insofar as Plato remained oriented toward Socratic discussion, and insofar as he recognizes our finitude and the consequent impossibility of systematizing language, he—unlike modern logicians—remains true to our original experience of language and the world that it constitutes. Put another way, he is far more "original" (*ursprünglich*) than Heidegger makes him out to be. Compare Heidegger, *Platons Lehre der Wahrheit* (Bern, 1954) and Gadamer, "Plato's Unwritten Dialectic." TRANSLATOR.

aneu pantōn autōn mathoi" ([we could] not learn any one [of them] by itself apart from all of them) (18c). However, as accords with their specific nature, they constitute a delimited realm even so, and thus they serve as an example for any technē (16c). Here, [knowledge of] the systematic structure (*desmos* [bond]) is tantamount to mastery of writing or of making music respectively. In regard to their structure, certainly, these two are the same as dialectic: ascent to the primary and descent from the primary belong together: "*touton ton desmon au logizamenos hōs onta hena kai panta tauta hen pōs poiounta*" (and we conceive of this, their bond, in turn as being one and somehow making all of them one and one into all of these) (18d). In each case the reference is plainly to a relative unity to which each tone or phoneme, respectively, belongs as such. Compare the parallel execution of *dihairein* (division), which departs from the one voice (*phōnē mia*) (17c) and, conversely, at 18b, from indeterminate voice (*phōnē aperios*). (The last approach seems easiest to Philebus, evidently because he follows the path of experience [18d].) Structurally, dialectic here corresponds closely to dialectic as it is portrayed at the conclusion of book 6 of the *Republic* (511b–c).

Of course, in the *Republic* the only archē spoken of is a single one, and there is no talk of relative first principles such as the principle of either voice or tone in the *Philebus*. That there is not would seem to signify that the examples in the *Philebus*—insofar as they involve something like tones or letters—must belong to what the *Republic* calls *dianoia*. Here, at 511c, the distinction between dianoia and dialectic still sets dialectic sharply apart from the "so-called technai," which do not justify their presuppositions. Only in the *Philebus* are technai such as music or the science of letters described in such a way that they themselves could be called dialectical. Does that not mean that Plato was indeed fully aware that the ideal of dialectical derivation of all things from a single archē could never be carried out completely?

An astonishing statement of Aristotle's would also seem to support this thesis. At the beginning of his ethics (*EN* 1095a32) he says that Plato considered it problematical whether one should work up toward the archai (first principles) or down from them. The plural is striking in itself. To be sure, it is characteristic of Aristotle's own use of language. But the aporia as such seems indicative of the fact that Plato did not envision a unified, fully elaborated deductive system. Otherwise it would not have been such an aporia at all. Furthermore, this aporia does indeed correlate with the examples of a two-sided procedure given in the description of the structure of technē in the *Philebus*. In "Plato's Unwritten Dialectic," I have attempted to clear up how the imperfectibility implied in Plato's doctrine of two principles— an imperfectibility that Aristotle elaborates for us—is reflected in Plato himself in the way indeterminate duality (*ahoristos dyas*) functions.

In any event, we are far removed here from Socrates' question about the good. This question arises as a question about aretē (virtue) and—given all the special forms of aretē—as a question about the aretai (virtues). And the aretai are not to be investigated in regard to universal considerations but rather in regard to the narrower realm of the good in human life. Certainly the most natural starting point for the question of the good is the good in human life. The program of the *Phaedo* addresses the good in human life, and so does the *Republic* when the question of the good is introduced there. And the same is true later when this question is raised again in the *Philebus*. But in all these cases the discussion transcends this narrower realm and leads to a universal ontological inquiry.

That it does so is not surprising if one remembers how universal the context was in which the question of the good is introduced in Plato's *Phaedo*—the context namely of inquiry into the cause of coming-into-being and pasing-away in general: "*holōs gar dei peri geneseōs kai phthoras tēn aitian diapragmateusas-thai*" (for it is appropriate to treat as a whole the cause of generation and destruction) (95e). Socrates advances his own example of knowledge of the good only as an illustrative introduction to the general question of what knowledge is. As early as the *Phaedo* a teleological cosmology is postulated, which, to be sure, is not worked out. Similarly, in the *Seventh Letter*, we find the extension of knowledge about aretē to knowledge about the whole of reality (344b). And, in the final analysis, the *Timaeus* is the mythical exposition of the unelaborated postulate of the *Phaedo*—even if, strictly speaking, the Socratic question is no longer mentioned there at all. One sees that Aristotle is extending a Platonic line of thought in his teleological physics and metaphysics. But how the widening of the agathon (good) to the *archē tōn pantōn* (principle of all things) is supposed to follow from the structure of dialectic is still obscure.

It seems to me that real clarification of this problem can be achieved only if one analyzes the actual procedure of dialectic, a procedure that is specified in the *Republic* only as a general program. We must find justification in this procedure of dialectic for the disquieting "in just the same way" that places the good alongside the other ideas. Let us remember that the underlying principle of Plato's utopian state (even in the first outlines of it) was to educate the guardians, in whose hands the power of government lay, to be immune to the seduction of power: in the end education *in* science was to be education *by* science. It is striking that in our passage, with its confusing "in just the same way," grasping the good is portrayed as the breakthrough that brings victory in battle. What battle? Against what enemy?[13]

13. The image Plato uses—which, of course, was suggested in particular by the warrior-guardian analogy of his utopia—in fact belongs to one self-con-

Obviously the concern is not only the abuse of power. Or, better said, even the abuse of power, which the constitution of a state is intended to prevent, derives from another fault. And Plato maintains that this other fault is a lack of dialectic, a lack of the art of differentiating. That, of course, sounds absurd. As if the passions which carry us away were forms of thinking, and all thinking were not overpowered precisely by the force of them! The *Protagoras* pushes this absurdity to the extreme: there, succumbing to the passions is said to be mere ignorance (352 ff.). This assertion notwithstanding, Plato's intellectualization of courage in book 4 of the *Republic* did disclose something important. He demonstrates convincingly that in regard to courage as a qualification for the warrior-guardians, the concern is that they hold fast to the right doxa (belief) about danger and not let themselves be dissuaded from that belief by anything—not even the seductive power contained in hēdonē (pleasure). That may indeed be expressed too "intellectually," and Aristotle, who always takes Plato word for word, accordingly discounts the Socratic position all too much when he comes to its aid with the argument that to some, a man might actually appear courageous only because they themselves overestimate the danger he faces (*EN* 1116b3 ff.). What Socrates has in mind is substantiated insofar as the issue is real political courage and not just physical courage (430b). For in political courage the concern is not so much the physical anxiety as such that overpowers us, as the rationalizations into which fear seduces us. And in the case of hēdonē the concern is even clearer: the seductive power of per-

---

tained semantic field: the expressions for logical operations are taken in large part from the language of wrestling and similar forms of fighting; so too, *aptōti* (not to be overthrown) in the passage here (cf. n. 8 above), and frequently *diamachesthai* (to fight hard, or contend), for instance, in the *Gorgias* at 503a and elsewhere.

suasion that emanates from hēdonē. To be sure, I cannot prove it in regard to this particular passage, but it seems clear to me that Plato is thinking of the flattery that legitimates the powerful in their abuse of their power. One need only recall the *Gorgias*, for instance, where the sophistic rhetorical art is portrayed as an art of flattery. We encounter something analogous here in the *Republic* when sophistic wisdom is likened to the art of comporting oneself properly toward a dangerous beast (493b). And in the depiction of how a youth (similar to Alcibiades) is lured away from dedication to philosophy and ruined, there is explicit reference to flattery, namely anticipatory flattery: "*prokolakeuontes tēn mellousan autou dynamin*" (flattering in advance a power he will yet have himself) (494c).

In any case it is true that whoever finds himself in the possession of power must fight his way through (*diamachesthai*) temptation in order not to succumb to the seduction of power. And anyone can see that such resistance is really an accomplishment of reason (*logos*) and, yes, even a question of reasonableness (*phronēsis*). In Plato's language reason and reasonableness are called dialectic, for his language usage is taken from [Socrates'] guiding of a discussion through all its episodes and gathering and holding together what is sought and actually meant through all the unsteadiness and errancy that pervade any discussion— be it with others or with oneself. Used this way, "dialectic" is, as we saw, not simply an art that can be learned. One succeeds in holding fast to what one sees before one's eyes as right not only logōi (in discourse) but also *ergōi* (in deed). Hence the guardians must be *monimoi*, steadfast—steadfast specifically in the sciences, just as in war and in everything else that is considered right (*en nomimois* [in lawful obligations]) (537d). The unerring way in which Socrates lived his life in Plato's portrayal of him— right up to the final temptation of the escape offered to him in the *Crito*—and, most of all, the long discussion as Socrates is taking leave of his friends in the *Phaedo* are the best illustrations of this steadfastness. An essential point that gives Plato's dialectic as a whole its underlying meaning is that he demands justification in logos from the persona of Socrates. For this reason—and not for reasons of aesthetics and taste[14]—it is vital to read Plato's dialogues not as theoretical treatises but as mimēsis (imitation) of real discussions played out between the partners and drawing them all into a game in which they all have something at stake.

In regard to the passage we are analyzing, it is indeed striking that the portrayal of the dialectician, who has the idea of the good before his eyes, puts particular emphasis on the struggle to withstand "tests" (*elenchoi*): "*hōsper en machēi dia pantōn elenchōn diexiōn*" (as if in battle, getting through all tests) (534c). Neither in reference to the mathematical studies that lead to "pure" thinking nor in reference to the universal requirement of giving justification for "being" was there any mention at all of tests. With what sovereignty are the *peri tauta deinoi* (the "experts" about these things) repudiated at 525d, for instance, when the doctrine of numbers is introduced! Plainly, the temptation to rationalize and the seductive sophistry of the passions play a special role in the matter of the good—and, one might certainly add, in the matter of the aretai, even the "intellectual" aretai, too. It is the role of what Kant calls a "natural dialectic" (*Foundations of a Metaphysics of Morals*, at the end of part 1).[15]

---

14. How astonishing that Gerhard Müller can hold that reading Plato's Socrates' mimēsis as mimēsis robs Plato's thinking of its seriousness (*Göttingische gelehrte Anzeigen*, vol. 229 (1975), pp. 157 ff.). What a degraded, aesthetical and mistaken concept of mimēsis, poetry, and myth!

15. Kant figures prominently in Gadamer's ethical thought. In "Über die Möglichkeit einer philosophischen Ethik," in *KS*, vol. 1, pp. 179–91 (henceforth

Thus one should take note that the portrayal of the dialectician here contains not only the word *elenchos* (test, refutation), which we know from the Socratic discussions, but a series of other words that we find in the later dialogues in the context of characterizing dialectic: *dihorisasthai, aphelein, diexienai,* to define thoroughly, to abstract, to run [get] through. "To define thoroughly" means to mark off one thing from another, hence, to differentiate. And that implies removing the thing meant from everything which is not meant (*abstrahere*) and getting through all differentiations until the end, that is, until an understanding is reached with others as well as oneself. The prefixes are of particular importance. The *dia* (through, thoroughly) implies at the same time an "asunder," hence a differentiation. And the *apo* (off, away) implies at the same time a "to," that is, a seeing together of what has been taken away. This vocabulary already anticipates the analyses of dialectic undertaken in the *Sophist* using the highest genera—being, identity, difference, and so forth. Here in the *Republic* the exposition still has a purely dialogical, indeed even military, timbre (*hōsper en machei* [as in a battle]). That does not happen by chance for the danger lurks in logos (discourse) itself.

Confusing something is the counterpart to distinguishing something, and the wrong separation is the counterpart to the right one. In confusing something and separating falsely, one

---

MPE), Gadamer attempts to develop an ethical theory in which Kant and Aristotle, far from being in conflict, complement each other. The application of practical reason in hitting the mean between the extremes in a particular situation can only succeed if reason is secured against the seductive influence of the desire for gratification and the "flattery" of the senses. For when reason is not so secured, it degenerates into rationalization. Gadamer reads Kant's *Foundations* as devoted primarily to this preparatory task of purifying the rational sense of duty from the subversive influence of the senses. TRANSLATOR.

gives oneself over to the play of opinions being bandied about. The counterpart to dialectic's getting through (*dia pantōn elenchōn* [through all tests]) is the dazzling art of the forceful answer (*kata doxan* [counter to what someone believes]), that is, the art of contradicting (*antilogikē technē*). In a word, the counterpart to dialectic is sophism. Sophism is a constantly threatening danger—something that can always happen to the logoi (assertions) "in us" ("*tōn logōn autōn athanaton ti kai agērōn pathos en hēmin*" (an experience in us, immortal and unaging, of the statements themselves) (*Philebus* 15d). Even in mathematics there are pseudo-proofs or pseudo-arguments which, as we know, Protagoras advanced in great number against mathematicians. Of course, Plato would say that someone who can really do mathematics is out of range of such rhetorical arts, even if the mathematician escapes simply by withdrawing from verbal disputes (*psiloi logoi* [vacuous arguments]) (*Theaetetus* 156a) and from Protagoras's entourage, as does Theodorus in the *Theaetetus*. On the other hand, where the subject is of the greatest importance, that is, in the realm of dialectic, one is threatened steadily by the danger of sophism. In the excursus of the *Seventh Letter*, this threat is explained in detail. But even where the "sophist" is firmly pinned down in a definition, as he is in the *Sophist* dialogue, his intrinsic proximity to the true dialectician and philosopher emerges. For merely clearing up how something has been mistaken for something it is not does not really put an end to the abuse of logos. This abuse is a *moral* matter.

Using the exemplary case of the *Lysis*, I have already elaborated in greater detail how Plato's early elenchtic dialogues are based entirely upon the correlation of logos (word) and ergon (deed) (see "*Logos* and *Ergon* in Plato's *Lysis*"). As a matter of fact, the connection between the logical and ethical aspects of true dialectic runs through the whole of Plato's work. And even

Aristotle confirms this correlation when he finds the difference between sophistry and philosophy to be purely the *prohairesis tou biou* (choice of the life [one leads]) (*Metaphysics* 1004b24; *Sophistical Refutations* 169b24, 171b8).

Thus it is not in the least remarkable that, in our passage, holding steadfast in the face of all confusion is emphasized especially in regard to the idea of the good. That it would be is already inherent in the whole utopian construction of the ideal state's constitution and of the education of the guardians which that constitution specifies. Hence, in the discussion of the educational program for these guardians, neither the content of the mathematical sciences nor the particular set of problems in the doctrine of ideas are under consideration as themes of dialectic. The sole interest is in turning the soul around toward noetic reality.

To be sure, when dialectic is raised out of, and beyond, mathematical dianoia in the *Republic*, we get a first hint that in the truly noetic realm—which has a presuppositionless (*anhypotheton*) archē, *that is, a principle preceding all hypothesis*—the concern will be the relationship of the ideas to each other. (And in an elaboration of that relationship, the inner unity in the structure of the mathematical disciplines would become transparent.) But this hint given at the end of book 6 is not pursued in what comes afterward, that is, in the interpretation and exposition of the allegory of the cave as a curriculum of education leading through mathematics and dialectic. And the "hyperbolic" position of the good, represented by the simile of the sun, is not really explained, as our detailed examination of the summary at 534b–c has shown. When it comes right down to it, the "ascent" to the noetic dimension is the single theme. Accordingly, the problem of participation, of methexis, which is so sharply disputed later on in the *Parmenides*, enters in here only insofar as it is said to be characteristic of the philosopher that he sees the beautiful itself and does not mix it up with the many beautiful things that "participate" in it. Here, methexis appears to imply only the differentiation of "it itself" from those things that participate in it. In other words, its reference is limited to what the *Phaedo* called the "simple" hypothesis of the eidos.

Significantly, when the "idea" is introduced explicitly in the *Phaedo*—perhaps for the first time in Plato's writings—it occurs for the stated purpose of putting a stop to the anti-logical arts of inducing confusion. The interpretation of the *Phaedo's* "hypothesis of the *eidos*" in recent Plato scholarship as a whole—and not only in the Marburg school's radicalization of the question—has kept its attention focused all too much on science. As a result, the ideas are taken to be the "tranquil realm of laws" (Hegel) that one approximates by critical testing of the hypotheses one postulates. But Plato did not have the process of scientific investigation in mind at all—rather, the sophistic abuse of that new marvel, an art of arguing able to confound any assertion: Socrates had been so confounded in his studies that in the end he no longer understood anything, not even what causes a human being to grow (96c). One has to read this text precisely: the hypothesis of the eidos is not to be tested against all-decisive "experience." The test of "experience" would be a complete absurdity for the postulation of an idea. What constitutes being a horse can never be confirmed or refuted by a single empirical horse. Rather, the test here relates to the immanent consistency of what the eidos comprises: one should not go a single step further until it is clear what such a postulation says in each case, and what it does not. Accordingly, one should note that it is not the hypothesis that gets tested against its consequences, but the presumed consequences that get tested against the hypothesis: everything that the hypothesis does not include should be ruled out. Above all, that means that the individual thing which participates in an eidos "counts" in an argument only in regard to the eidos in which it participates, that is, only in regard to its essential, eidetic content. All logical confusion has its origin in not keeping the eidos separate from what only participates in it. For if one fails to keep these separate, one easily gets entangled in contradictions, such as saying that the number two "comes into being" both by addition and by division. A proper testing of the hypothesis of the eidos repudiates as sophistic all adulteration introduced here by the concept of "coming into being." (A good illustration of this function of the hypothesis, *Republic* 525d, has been treated above.)

The portrayal [of this procedure] in the *Phaedo* is obviously intended to be of the highest formal generality: the illustration given is the noetic example of the number. Even so, what is said here is in complete accord with the demand made of the philosopher in the *Republic*, that he differentiate the eidos from everything that participates in it. Of course, one must be clear that this procedure of hypothesizing the eidos is only the preliminary precondition of all argumentation, only the first step which provides an initial foothold on the shaky ground of the logoi. No knowledge is attained by this procedure yet. As early as the *Phaedo*, no doubt is left about that. And to this extent there never was such a thing as Plato's "Eleaticism": the schema of "development" in Plato proposed by Stenzel—from aretē to dihairesis—which, per se, contains many correct observations must be qualified accordingly. In the *Phaedo* only the application of the procedure of hypothesis to the immortality of the soul and the comparison of the soul to snow, which disappears when the fire of the sun warms it, is supposed to yield anything like knowledge.

Nevertheless, this first step on the path of dialectic lays the foundation. It is the step into the noetic realm as such, a step that is presupposed whenever one is serious about giving justification. When Plato describes dialectic in the *Republic*, its differentiating is played out entirely in the noetic sphere (511c). We will see later in our analysis of the *Philebus* that there, too, this first step of reflection, the step into the noetic, is taken explicitly. There, Protarchus names the contradictions that result from the correlativity of the one and the many and, similarly, of the large and the small—contradictions that are introduced in the *Republic* (523a ff.) expressly as the "call" to awaken to thinking. In the *Philebus* (14d) Protarchus has to be told by Socrates that these contradictions are trite and overworked. Matters only become serious once *noetic* unities are under consideration, and when *these* are said to be one and many at the same time. And in what follows, the dialectical nature of all science is founded on this noetic basis. Even in the very words he uses here, Plato is opposing true dialectic to the art of confounding someone: for example, in the *Phaedo*, 101e, "*phyroio*" (would confuse), and in the *Philebus*, 15d–e, "*symphyron*" (confusing).

IV

THE DIALECTIC OF THE GOOD
IN THE *PHILEBUS*

Of all Plato's dialogues, the *Philebus* has long been considered the most important source we possess for the mysterious Platonic doctrine of the ideal numbers. Of course, this aspect of the dialogue should not concern us, given the context of our present investigation. Our question is the reverse one: what relationship, if any, does this doctrine, known to us above all from Aristotle, have to the Socratic question *about aretē and the human good*? Put another way, what was Plato thinking of when he took up the principles of the one and the indeterminate two in his famous public lecture "On the Good," and then nevertheless came to speak in it of human virtues?[1] The *Philebus* must contain an answer to this question, for in no other dialogue of Plato's is the theory of dialectic so tightly interwoven with the dialectic of human practice. The "transitions" in this dialogue pose a long-standing and famous problem. But of primary importance here is the fact that the Socratic question about the good in human life is actually posed again, and yet in such a way that, simultaneously, the universal nature of the good is always kept in view. Similarly, the nature of dialectic is treated in statements of the utmost generality and universality—albeit without any mention of the good per se in these reflections which are specifically said

1. See Aristotle's gloss in the *Magna Moralia*, cited below, ch. 5, n. 3.

to concern the principles of dialectic. Instead, the universal question about the good is woven completely into the plot of the discussion, that is, the dispute about the respective importance to human life of hēdonē and phronēsis.

Thus here we find together again all those things that in the *Republic* got dispersed over the wide-ranging considerations of Socrates' long discussion of the true state: the Socratic question about the good, the doctrine of the ideas and their dialectic, and the doctrine of the uppermost principle, that is, the good. And all this occurs in a discussion between Socrates and quite young people, whom he must introduce to these things *ab ovo*.

And indeed, here in the *Philebus* the question that we found posed in the *Republic*—whether pleasure or thinking is the highest good (505b)—is made the theme of a dramatic confrontation. The advocates of pleasure are no longer dismissed from the start as they were in the *Republic*. After all, in defending their position they can summon in support a truly important trait of life that pervades all living things. Behind these advocates stands, we suspect, the figure of Plato's great friend, the mathematician and scholar Euduxus, to whom Aristotle later makes respectful reference in the same context (*EN*, Kappa 2). Those who advocate "thinking" will have to justify their claim that it is supreme against this universal principle of life that pervades even the human being, who is distinct by virtue of memory, deliberation, and the like. At first it seems as if two irreconcilable basic attitudes were being pitted against each other here. For just as it steers the behavior of any living thing, the pleasure principle has a kind of obvious predominance, unlimited and overpowering, in the human being too. That one should argue for this principle in [rational] statement and answer would seem to be self-contradictory, and hence it is entirely consistent that those who do advocate it do indeed resist giving justification of their position in this way. The most visible indication of this reluctance is the fact that Philebus, in whose honor the dialogue is named, withdraws from the discussion entirely.

Thus there is good reason for why the old Socratic question of the good in human life leads precisely at this point to thematizing the dialectical principle of giving justification. Resistance to the demand that justification be given is part and parcel of the hedonist position. Philebus is consistent when he does not oppose this demand with a logical argument but, instead, dogmatically insists on the unconditional priority of hēdonē: "That's what I believe and that's what I always will believe" (*dokei kai doxai*) (12a). He bids adieu to the whole thing in order not to do any harm to his "goddess" Pleasure by accepting any uncomfortable assumptions about her. And when Socrates gives a demonstration of the principle of differentiation, illustrating it with examples of particular technai [grammar and harmony], Philebus cannot see what that could possibly have to do with his contention, of which he is so completely certain (18a–b). The allusion is the same at 22c, where we find, "and not your *nous* (reason) either!" In this phrasing, "your reason" (*ho sos nous*) (22c), we detect—even in the negative— Philebus's absolute partiality for his goddess Hedone. Philebus's intransigence is made all the more evident by the skirmishing in which Socrates defends the official cult name, Aphrodite, against *Philebus*['s attempts to rename her] (12c). Philebus wants to consecrate Hedone artificially. Socrates, in contrast, stays with the cult name for Aphrodite—that is to say, he recognizes her as a member of the Olympian family of gods. In substance, his doing so establishes the merely partial validity and limits of hēdonē's claim to be the dominant power in the world. After that Philebus allows himself to open his mouth just once more, and then solely to reinforce that no limits can be set to the desire for pleasure (27e—as in Nietzsche's "for all pleasure wants eternity").

Protarchus, who takes over Philebus's part, is now introduced step by step to the process[2] of giving justification. As his initiation proceeds, the structure of dialectic is simultaneously clarified. At first he resists any differentiating among pleasures: as pleasure, he says, they are all one and the same thing (12b and 13c). Socrates counters with the example of the genus color and points out that to insist on the mere unity of the genus is to say nothing at all. On the contrary, at the moment when one wants to say anything about a genus—for instance, that it is good—one must differentiate. Precisely in order to escape the sheer irrationality (*alogia*) of such all-inclusive arguments that run everything together, Socrates develops the dialectic of the one and the many—a dialectic implicit in the postulation of any such ideal generic unit. He sees an abuse of this dialectic precisely here, where the principle of hēdonē is defended by means of such an all-inclusive reduction. When he goes on to demonstrate what for him is the productive application of differentiation, using convincing examples, his partner does accede, but then tries one last objection: Is there, he asks, really a need for such subtle dif-

---

2. *Bewegung*. The word figures prominently in the Hegelian tradition and means primarily motion or movement, not in the spatial but in the logical-developmental sense. Hegel wishes to trace the "movement" of the "concept" or subject matter (*Sache*) of thought, as it unfolds itself. Gadamer finds this same attention to the self-unfolding of the subject matter in Plato's dialogical art, the only difference being that Plato stays much closer to the discursive character of our thinking and speaking. For Gadamer, every discussion, if we are willing to submit ourselves to it, takes its own course, and the task is thus to let the thing under discussion display itself apart from any arbitrary intrusions (Hegel: *Einfälle*) in the process. See "Hegel and the Dialectic of the Ancient Philosophers," in *HD* pp. 5–34. TRANSLATOR.

ferentiations in the types of pleasure and thinking, when the issue is as existentially important as the question of the good? Protarchus is speaking quite Socratically here: one should not remain hidden to oneself, he says (19c). But paradoxically, he says this in order to evade Socrates' demand that he pursue the dialectic—a highly ingenious, ironic twisting by Plato of existential seriousness and the dialectical game. Socrates is surprisingly willing to go along with seeking an alternative approach to resolving the dispute. As he so often does, he introduces an argument quite on the sly, which, when all is said and done, will serve to support his thesis, which here is to prove the priority of nous over hēdonē. The argument is the doctrine of the four genera (23b ff.). From this point on, his partner goes along with him ever more readily, no longer allowing himself to be misled even by Philebus's final intervention (28b). Something quite surprising now happens: when the doctrine of the four genera is applied to the two contestants, hēdonē and nous, hēdonē is assigned *in toto* to [the first genus,] the apeiron (indeterminate), and nous to the fourth, the aitia (cause). With this conclusion the argument might be considered settled. But instead, Socrates asks where and in what way (*en hōi te kai dia ti pathos*) these two, hēdonē and phronēsis, show up in the visible realm (31b). And from this moment on, no more persuasion is needed to involve his partner in more and more subtle, and further and further differentiated, analysis of the most varied forms in which hēdonē appears (and later, phronēsis too).

This transition is the least obtrusive, yet perhaps also the most important of all in this dialogue, which is so rich in transitions. The transition here to the concrete manifold of experience takes place automatically, so to speak. And the application of the procedure of differentiation, which Protarchus had shied away from before, now takes place automatically too, and with his willing assistance (32c).

It is remarkable how this "guiding of the soul" (*psychagōgē*) is combined with highly theoretical expositions of the principles of dialectic. Socrates—in his typically secretive, oracular way— supports his argument with appeals to obscure sources of knowledge and even vague dreams. Plainly he makes no claim that what he says is authoritative. Rather, he sets the listener free once again to recognize himself in what is said.[3] In this way Socrates does indeed get his partner to enter into the dialectical movement voluntarily.

After all, dialectic, as the art of differentiating rightly, is really not some kind of secret art reserved for philosophers. Whoever is confronted with a choice must decide. Being confronted with choices, however, is the unalterable circumstance of human beings. Their having to make choices removes them from the realm of the rest of living things, which unquestioningly follow their animal desires (*thērion erōtes*) (67b) wherever these—like forces of nature—may drive them. To be a human being means always to be confronted with choices. As Aristotle puts it, human beings "have" *prohairesis* (choice). They must choose. Having to choose, however, entails wanting to know, that is, to know what is best, to know what is good. And that means knowing reasons why, knowing grounds, and using grounds to differentiate. Socrates' partners in the discussion experience this: they learn

---

3. Gadamer maintains that Plato's myths are a sort of mirror in which we are meant to recognize ourselves. (See ch. 2. n. 9, on self-knowledge and the Socratic *gnōthi s'auton*.) Their validity, accordingly, is not dependent upon any authorities to whom they might appeal, but upon their pertinence and accuracy in portraying the phenomena of human existence, and their efficacy in helping one to achieve self-knowledge. TRANSLATOR.

that concern for a life of justice and rectitude necessarily leads to giving justification for the good.

Thus, the opening scene, in which the two ideals pleasure and knowledge are opposed to each other, is already pervaded by a latent contradiction. The way in which all living things blindly submit to the immediacy of the pleasure principle—driven as they are by the hidden power of the life urge—is not the way for human beings to fulfill their potential for leading their own life. Hence, right from the start, the exposition of the question is such that a contradiction must ultimately emerge, namely that here one of the options supposedly open to choice can in fact not be chosen at all. The blindness of the life urge, which prevails in everything, exists completely apart from any choice. The other "choice" or option balancing the blind life urge is choosing itself—for which one has already decided *as soon as one begins weighing these two against each other*. And this choice presupposes knowledge. What makes human beings human beings is the fact that they must ask about the good and must give preference to one thing over another (*prohairein*) in conscious, deliberate decision. In other words, they must give themselves justification (*Apology* 38a).

Protarchus outgrows his immature dependence on Philebus and his partisan support of him. He develops into Socrates' candid partner. At the beginning he just goes along with the differentiating. At the end his thirst to know is such that he will not let go of Socrates. Socrates leads the discussion through the differentiation of various kinds of pleasure and knowledge. The task then—after it has been settled that neither one of these two by itself can constitute the good life—is to "mix" the proper portion of each correctly in the right life. That, of course, is a metaphor. Life is treated like a potion in which various ingredients are to be mixed to achieve blended, full-bodied tastiness. Selecting the right ingredients and combining them well obviously presupposes the good as the standard to which one refers. That is to say, one mixes with a view to the [harmoniousness and consonance] of the whole. The important thing is that we be able to gather from the metaphor what makes the mixture "good."

We should not let ourselves be led astray by the metaphor. We are, of course, not dealing here with a real mixture of substances that are found separately from each other. Such talk is merely the language of a simile, as is expressly stated at 59e. Both ingredients exist solely in logos (reasoning). Would pleasure be anything at all without consciousness, without our being aware of it? And pure absorption in knowing—insofar as it is a total loss of oneself to what is thought—would fall just as short of being life. Even Aristotle's god "enjoys" his vision. Hence, here in Plato, self-knowledge is concealed on both sides of this abstract antithesis, that is, self-knowledge that alone, obviously, can make both sides desirable in the first place. Given the hiddenness of this self-knowledge, we also see why only a joining of both sides, of knowing and perception on the one hand and pleasure on the other, can display the sole thing in concrete human life that is desirable—the human good.

From the beginning, something is evident here which is ever more firmly established as the discussion proceeds, namely, that the good life must consist in a third thing, a mixed genus in which hēdonē and "limitless drives," on the one hand, and reason (*nous*) as the source of all measuring and measured restraint, on the other, are both found. Certainly we should not take this metaphor to mean that the mixture is real and can be brought about properly by some kind of art (technē) of living. Unlike an artisan who is smart at selecting his materials, we do not stand at a distance from the components of our life, our drives and our intelligence. On the contrary, we ourselves *are* both of these.

Plato knows how to indicate this fact. He finds an ingenious way to momentarily suspend his technē analogy of making a mixture. He has Socrates insist that the question be put to both manifolds—of pleasure and of knowing—to what extent each will accept the other side. In truth they are both only abstract aspects of the one life we really live, the life that is both; and our task is to inquire how this one life unfolds itself (63a).

There is an implication here, however: put in the language of the likeness, if the good life is to be the most beautiful and the most free of inner discord, what is good about it—"good" in the same sense in human beings and in the cosmos (*en t'anthrōpōi kai tōi panti pephyken agathon*)—must be comprehended, and also the idea (*idea*) of that good (64a). Even if one grasps the mixture metaphor in this way as an image of real human self-knowledge, the question about the good, about its normative role in this mixture, remains. Indeed, it becomes more acute than ever. Consequently, we cannot escape having to articulate conceptually here what we call good in regard to this mixture, which is to say, what we call good in regard to our concrete human existence.

We now see the actual meaning of that mysterious doctrine of the four genera. It is obviously an extension of the Pythagorean doctrine of opposites, the peras (limit) and the apeiron (limitless, indefinite), and it is introduced as such. But there is something new: Plato, namely, is not simply a Pythagorean. On the contrary, he explicitly distinguishes the noetic world of numbers and mathematical relationships from what is given in the reality of concrete appearances. The latter he calls "*genesis*" (becoming). Genesis does not identify still another form of ideal being *but rather the "real" being of what comes to be*. There "is" the reality of the genus of things mixed from the peras and the apeiron [the reality of genesis] just as there "is" [the eidetic reality of] the peras and apeiron themselves (and just as there "is" necessarily a cause for the third, mixed genus). Not only hēdonē and *lypē* (pain) appear in this mixed genus of the "real" (31c). In a decisive passage it is emphasized that the good is to be sought here too (61b). At issue, to be sure, is solely the good in human life. The good in human life, however, is just as much the good in the state and in the cosmos too. That the good is the same in all three is confirmed when Plato reminds us of *hygeia* (health) and *harmonia* (harmony) and points out their cosmic relevance (for example, at 31c). The doctrine of the four genera thus proves to be both the ontological preparation for, and prerequisite of, the debate in the *Philebus*. Only when the mixture is no longer thought of as a diminution and clouding of the pure, true, and unmixed, but as a genus of its own, can it be the place where we see how the being of the good and the true is constituted. In this way we arrive at the metaphor of the potion of life: the way is prepared for it ontologically by the differentiation of the four genera of being.

This doctrine has far-reaching consequences for any appropriate understanding of Plato's dialectic and of the problems of chōrismos (separation) and methexis (participation). If limit and determinacy do not exist apart, for themselves, then neither does the entire noetic realm of the ideas—any more than do the ingredients of this potion of life that is supposed to be mixed. That the noetic world of numbers and pure relationships belongs together with their dialectical opposite, the apeiron, implies that they are only abstracted aspects of this third thing called the "mixed" (*ex amphoin symmisgomenon, meikton* [combined from both, mixed]) (23d, 25b). It is established expressly at 27b that our life—this life, mixed from pleasure and knowledge—belongs in the third genus. But that it does is, after all, virtually self-evident. It was indeed difficult for Protarchus to grasp this third genus and precisely because it is ubiquitous: "Its numerousness (*plē-thos*) startled you" (26c). Plato is pointing to a self-evident truth, namely, the obvious fact that the particular participates in the universal. After the confusions of a dialectic of making one many and vice versa, a dialectic that ended in vacuity, the third genus of the mixed now appears as the reality, or being, that has come into being (*gegenēmenē ousia*) (27b). The fourth genus, the "cause" of the mixture, makes clear that this third genus is a genus of its own and is not to be derived from the eidetic opposition of peras and apeiron, but is instead a special kind of being.

The doctrine of the four aspects of being developed here is a universal ontological doctrine, which is to say, that it extends far beyond the particular occasion for which it was introduced here—namely, the question of the good in human life—and embraces the whole cosmos and its constitution. We may go even further: nowhere in the entirety of Plato's dialogues are we as close as we are here to Aristotle's parallel account of the two principles, the one and indeterminate duality. If one starts here in Plato, even something like a physics—that is, an eidetic science of what, in its essence, coming-into-being is—no longer seems completely impossible. Coming-into-being, becoming, is, after all, becoming being. It is being that has come to be. Even so, the Socratic question about the good in human life is included here too. Physics and ethics can still appear here, undifferentiated from each other, as mere applications of the basic ontological structure of the good. And the mode of discourse that is used here to describe both these ways in which the good appears, could, if viewed in relation to Aristotle's technique of conceptualization, be termed mythical. A world whose origination and determinate order are caused and executed by a master craftsman who possesses reason, or a human life whose ingredients are knowledgeably and expertly combined into a blended potion by an ideal drink-mixer—these are mythical metaphors. And it seems to me that Aristotle's physics and ethics achieve a translation of them into concepts.

If the good is accepted as the cause of any mixture being good—and ultimately this means, as the cause of everything real being good (64d)—the famous "beyond all being" (*epeikena tēs ousias*) takes on a new meaning. *The good is no longer the one.* On the contrary, it is explicitly conceived of according to the ideal of mixture and as having *three* aspects (*syntrisi* [in three together]). The dynamis (power) of the good has taken refuge in the *physis* (nature) of the beautiful: measure and measuredness constitute what beauty and aretē are everywhere (*"metriotēs gar kai symmetria, kallos dēpou kai aretē pantachou symbainei gignesthai"*) (64e).

We are far removed here from some esoteric, abstract, dialectical doctrine. It is stated expressly that all human beings know what is meant (64d). For this reason there is no terminological precision in this description whatsoever. Beauty, symmetry or measuredness, and truth (*alētheia*) are named as the three structural components of the good, which appears as the beautiful.

Thus, in the intrinsic connection between the good and the beautiful, which is brought out so emphatically here, we can see an indication that "the good," which is at the same time "the beautiful," does not exist somewhere apart for itself and in itself, somewhere "beyond." Rather, it exists in everything that we recognize as a beautiful mixture. What is viewed from the perspective of the *Republic* (or the *Symposium*) as the pure unmixed good or beautiful "beyond being" is here determined to be the structure of "the mixed" itself. In each case it would seem to be found only in what is concretely good and beautiful. And precisely the unity and integration of the appearance itself would thus appear to constitute its being good. This thesis, it seems to me, does not represent a change in Plato's teaching, a change that would have led him to abandon the doctrine of ideas or the transcendence of the good. It is still true that the good must be separated out of everything that appears good and seen in distinction from it. But it is in everything and is seen in distinction from everything only because it is in everything and shines forth from it.

The *Phaedrus* already points us decisively in this direction when its grand myth about the divine gift of erōs (love) singles out beauty as the only idea that preserves something of the former lustrousness of an idea even after our plunge into this earthly world. Beauty lights up here in our world. It shines forth most of all, and it, most of all, stimulates love in us (*ekphanesta-ton [esti] kai erasmiōtaton*) (*Phaedrus* 250c). Thus it awakens in the lover the longing and passion for what is higher. To say that, of course, is not to provide a conceptual answer to the problem of the participation of the particular in the universal. But it is nontheless significant that beauty is singled out because it "shines forth." For after all, that means that it is *in* the visible. Actually the beautiful, as the thing which is loved, is surpassingly "pure" beauty. It stands fully visible in its lustrousness. Being beautiful (*kalos*) means in the first place being presentable and refers to what can be seen in public. (Cf. the *Philebus* 65e, on the ugly (*aischron*), which "we keep hidden out of sight" (*aphani-zontes kryptomen*).) Thus, if we start with the *Phaedrus*, we can understand what is meant when it is said that the good's capacity to be, its potential (*dynamis*), is displayed in the beautiful. Of it-self and according to its own nature (*tautēn esche moiran* [hav-ing this destiny]) (250d), the good is appearance (*erscheinen*), lighting up (*aufscheinen*), shining forth (*herausscheinen*, or in Greek, *ekphainesthai*).[4]

---

4. This Heideggerian play on words is meant seriously. The root verb, *scheinen*, corresponds to *phainesthai* in Greek, whence the noun *phainomenon*.

Thus, out of the rushing flood of the audible, the numerically determinate relationship of the "pure tones" comes to the fore—harmony in music. Or, in their function as letters, determinate lines of script emerge from the whole of the visible, and phonemes from the rest of what is to be heard, each as the special articulation of meaning that it is. Similarly, that which lives is brought forth as an organic body (*Philebus* 29d), and the entire universe as a harmonic order. These are raised out of the limitless flowing away of mere genesis and are raised up into ousia (being). Its having been raised to ousia constitutes the intelligibility (*nous*), or dis-concealedness (*alētheia*), of the cosmic order. In all these instances the eidetic-ideal can be discerned, picked out, because it is contained in them (*heurēsein gar enousan* [for (it is) to be found existing therein]) (16d).

That the good has sheltered itself in the beautiful thus means nothing less than that it is to be found only in the beautiful. Measure, symmetry, and openness to view (*alētheia*) characterize the beautiful. To this extent the beautiful is at the same time the good, which provides everything that is with its true being— with the being, namely, that we have called here eidetic-ideal.

The dynamis of the good had already been spoken of in the *Republic*, and it was also said there that the good provides everything with its alētheia. Here the good "appears" precisely as the beautiful. It is in no way separable from that which it is in each instance. That it is not is vouched for by Plato's language. The language of the *Philebus*, to be sure, might indeed be nonterminological. Still, I would call to mind how the puzzling nature of dynamis is characterized in the *Republic*—not as existing apart

---

Phainomena are not "mere appearances," but the ways in which a thing really displays itself. Compare *SZ*, pp. 28–31, on phenomenology as the art of letting a thing show up, forth, and so forth, in discursive exposition. TRANSLATOR.

for itself, but "in that in which it exists and which it effects" (*eph' hōi te esti kai hōi apergazetai*) (*Republic* 477c–d). That holds universally. Hence, one must look for the dynamis of the good in the manifold of what the dynamis of the good brings about—as, for instance, the dynamis of seeing consists in the manifold of sights and nothing else. In conceptual language, that means that we are dealing here with the inseparability of the one from the many. True reality, or "being," is one but nevertheless in all the many things. And that means that it is separated from itself "which, however, seems to be the most impossible thing of all" (*Philebus* 15b). Since it is one and the same in many things that are separate from each other, it is simultaneously in them completely, and hence it is separate from itself. This circumstance is the seemingly nonsensical state of affairs with which Socrates is confronted in the *Parmenides*. He seeks a way out by referring to the light of day, which is everywhere at once and yet one and the same, not separated from itself (131b). In the *Parmenides*, of course, he does not succeed in keeping a proper hold on his thesis. He is still too young. But in the *Philebus*, Socrates characterizes precisely this problem as the source of all perplexity (*aporia*) if it is not properly allowed for, and the way to all felicitous advance (*euporia*) if it is (*Philebus* 15c).

And in fact the felicitous, good way of reaching an understanding, which the discussion in the *Philebus* traverses, gets completely beyond the danger that Socrates had warned against at the beginning, namely, the eristic tricks of sophistic pseudo-dialectic. This sophistic dialectic is not real thinking, for in pursuing it one succumbs to the blind desire for success in contentious argument: "*hyph' hēdonēs enthousiai te kai panta kinei logon asmenos*" (enthused with pleasure he delightedly sets every sort of argument in motion) (15e).

To be sure, the way toward reaching an understanding and

making sense of things that the discussion pursues—the path of first differentiating and then finally coming to a decision by weighing what is to be allowed and what rejected—does not fit all that well with the theoretical reflection that Socrates initiates via this path. The examples that he uses, music and letters, have to do with differentiations of voice or, better said, articulations that constitute a system. All singing and all speaking are based upon the intelligible lawfulness of the respective musical and linguistic uses of voice. Insight into this lawfulness is technē. But what is produced on the basis of this technē or skill—the musical mimēsis (imitation) or the speech content, say in persuasion, instruction, or poetry—could surely be brought about by some other, quite different technē too. For example, one might think here of the true rhetoric in the *Phaedrus*, as opposed to mere "grammar," this general skill which, in Plato, hovers in a remarkable way somewhere in between the articulation of letters and the articulation of the spoken voice. Grammar is presupposed in any discussion (and in any dialogue that is given literary form), and ultimately in any thinking at all that differentiates. In this sense it also plays a valid role, of course, in the search for the right life portrayed in the *Philebus*. But those in search of the right life are not on the good dialectical path to reaching a genuine understanding about the good just because they have learned to speak or write. The path one takes in search of the truth is plainly dialectic in a different sense from the dialectic of the arts of speaking or writing.

The two senses of dialectic may have something in common, namely, the division of a one into a determinate manifold that is itself eidetic-ideal. In the language of logic we would speak here of the unit of the genus and the manifold of species and subspecies in which this generic unit is specified. Also, one might grant that the number has a general paradigmatic function [in both cases]. After all, the art of differentiating only reaches its goal when one finds no more specifiable units—tones, phonemes, and so forth. So one might see in all dialectical division of a one into many a certain approximation to Plato's coordination of idea and number.

Differentiation takes place here within the noetic one, and it is the principle of number that the *Philebus* introduces in this context as the truly illuminating Promethean fire. Here, the Pythagorean heritage, the identification of being with number, is explicated on the new level of noetic being. In this way the multiplicity that the one contains receives numerical determination. It is many but not indefinitely many, rather so and so many. The numerical determination of what constitutes tones and tonal relationships in music, this ancient Pythagorean inheritance, has its correlate in the ideality of language and writing, both of which articulate the whole of human phonemes and, by doing so, put them at our disposal.[5]

Hence it is an eidetic-ideal structure, a relationship of *ideas*, that underlies the knowledge and skill in which any technē consists. This ideality certainly does not eliminate technē's relationship to the production of something in perceptible reality, for example, tones and music or articulated speech and what is fixed in writing. But the thing produced in this way retains a special kind of ideality itself. It is a world of signs and indices that directs us to the ideal. Accordingly we are not dealing here with just any particular handcraft among many others, one that Plato would say is less a technē than a mere routine (*tribē*). Rather, we have here two arts which were later called "free" (*liberales*) because

---

5. Even within the book of aporiai at *Metaphysics*, Beta 4, 999b30, the ideality of letters becomes clear, and this ideality entails that they have an ideal universality which takes multiple forms in the individual instances to which they are applied.

each in its own way is subordinate to no particular aims, and because each is so comprehensive.

Now the mixing of the potion of life also has an inclusive, universal aspect. The ingredients, which one after the other, are found acceptable for the mixture, have something to do with number insofar as the examination and testing of them is supposed to be comprehensive and exhaustive, *that is, is supposed to include just the right number of them*. Nevertheless, the thought here cannot be that one learns how to live in the right way, and is finally capable of it, in the manner in which one learns how to sing, speak, or write.

Or should we say only that one learns about the right and just life in the way one learns about giving justification for something and in the end is finally able to give it? But that is just what the discussion [in the *Philebus*] teaches us: dialectic is not a technē that one learns like writing, not something that others (illiterates) cannot do. Thinking, to be sure, is an art, but an art that is practiced by everyone and that one is never finished learning. And how to live is just as little an art that one could ever be finished learning. Futhermore, right thoughts about life and the idea of the right and just life—the highest thing that one could learn (*megiston mathēma*)—only become visible in general outlines *and not in regard to specifics (cf. Aristotle, *EN* 1098a21)*. Aristotle knows that the theoretical reflections that he calls "ethics" have to be of use in life as it is actually lived. Similarly, it is clear to Plato and to the reader of the *Philebus* that what results from this dialogue, the ideal of a life harmonized rightly, is—precisely as the result of dialogue—a logos (statement in words), which directs us to an ergon (deed), to choosing what is right in the moment of choice.

This is not the place to pursue the intrinsic connections between the dialectic of the one and the many and the doctrine of the ideal numbers. Of interest to us here is only the fact that human life, just as all other being, belongs to the mixed genus, and that what is called "being-good" appears in the reality of what is mixed. That it does so must mean that everything that exists has reality only in its concrete determinacy. And that means precisely that it is set in, and surrounded by, the unlimitedly variable—genesis. Similarly the conduct of human life that is guided by practical reason, also has the good in it only insofar as the good is concretized in the actual doing of it, that is, in giving preference to one thing over another (*prohairesis*). That would mean too that any deed, to the extent that it is decision, always includes a component of uncertainty, for it must move in an element that exceeds all determinacy and delimitation, which is therefore called "*apeiron*" (indefinite).

Consequently, human life is *eo ipso* dialectical.[6] It is one and many at the same time. At every moment it is itself and, exactly for that reason, separated from itself, just as the "what-it-is" (*ti estin*) of every existent thing ultimately exists in such a way that it is in all that participates in it (*to metechon*). The aporiai for-

6. The use of the word *dialectic* in Gadamer shifts. Here the reference is to the inner tension in human existence between order and disorder, the rational and the bestial. Our task is to maintain unity of self, integrity, within ever threatening disintegration into boundless chaos. Thus we must be constant in holding to one thing (Kierkegaard) through the vicissitudes of our life (cf. *PDE* and ch. 1, n. 22) Dialectic in this sense also has to do with dialogue insofar as the Socratic "art" of leading a discussion is an "art" of keeping it from getting lost in the indefiniteness of many things that are not important and of holding to the one thing that is—the one subject matter under discussion. Gadamer shows that phronēsis is the requisite virtue for both these forms of constancy in holding to one definite thing within threatening indeterminacy—in moral practice and in discussion. And it is the "dialectical" nature of its content in both these applications that distinguishes phronēsis from any technē whose content is a systematic whole that we could ever be finished learning. TRANSLATOR.

mulated in the *Philebus* are to be taken literally. They are not contradictions but the path taken by thinking itself.

Though the perspective is somewhat different, this doctrine of human existence, it seems to me, is also reflected in the *Statesman*, a doctrine which so decisively preempts Aristotle's criticisms. In the *Statesman* a distinction is made between a relative art of measurement (*Messen*) and an art of measurement that takes what is fitting (*angemessen*) as its measuring rod. The relative art of measurement knows only what is more, relative to what is less or vice versa. The true art of measurement, for which what is "fitting" is the measure, knows a "more" that is not only a "more" relative to a "less" but is really (*hōs on*) more (*Statesman* 284a). With such knowledge, this art of measurement brings about what is fitting: "*pros tēn tou metriou genesin*" (in regard to establishing what is fitting) (284c). Even without going further into the context in which the distinction between these two occurs, we can say that, viewed ontologically, "the fitting" (*to metrion*) here is what is called "the mixed" in the *Philebus*—namely, everything that has to do with what is fitting or appropriate, with the right moment, the obligatory (*to deon*)—in short, with what is in the middle between the extremes (284e–f.). Here one finds precisely the fundamental concepts of Aristotle's ethics. Though we must concede that the Socratic concern for one's own soul is extended by Plato's Socrates into the realm of the political-utopian and cosmic-universal, we see, nonetheless, that the Socratic question also lives on even here where the universal doctrine of ideas and the universal nature of dialectic are under discussion. That, more than anything else, is what the *Philebus* teaches us.

One must view what results here in relationship to the "transcendence" of the good that the *Republic* emphasizes so strongly. Though it is not easy to grasp just how it happened, that which makes all good things good found itself expelled there from the ranks of what exists. It is not one thing alongside of others; "it itself," *auto to agathon* (the good itself), withdraws. The good is the being of the ideas generally and not an idea itself.

I hope to have made credible that this way of putting things is simply the mythical form in which Plato expresses essentially the same thing that he says explicitly in the *Philebus* when he states that the good "appears" in the beautiful. And I would like to show that the problem that Plato's mythical question about the good contains is the same one that Aristotle later singles out as the problem of analogy or the *analogia entis*.[7] The transcendence of the good precludes thinking of it as an idea—a ti estin—that would constitute the highest, all-comprehensive genus, so to speak. But if this is so, neither the being of the good nor the being of any ti estin needs to be mediated with what exists in order to be like what exists—whatever form that mediation might take, for example, specification, diahairesis, or any other form of dividing up the whole. It cannot be mediated in this way at all; it appears in existence *im*mediately. That is the meaning of the statement that the good takes refuge in the beautiful. Thus, to my way of thinking, the result of our investigation of the special status of the idea of the good in Plato's works would seem to be that Plato's so-called self-criticism, as one is wont to interpret his *Parmenides*, is a criticism that we would be better off applying to ourselves. In the final analysis, our wanting to think of the participation of existent things in being as a relationship of existent things to each other always involves us in a false concretion. In-

7. Compare E. Frank, *Wissen, Wollen, Glauben* (Zurich, 1955), pp. 86–119.

stead we would do better to acknowledge from the start that this participation is the point of departure for all meaningful talk of the idea and of the universal.

Whoever seeks to conceive of the transcendent nature of the good cannot think of it as "a good." On the contrary, he will have to consider the three levels in the order of reality: the soul, the state, and the world—an order that is explicated mythically in Plato's dialogues, above all in the *Republic* and the *Timaeus*. It is not their beauty alone that constitutes the unity of unity and multiplicity which appears visibly in these things. Rather, it is the dynamis of the good, which holds everything together everywhere and gathers everything together into a unity.

V

ARISTOTLE'S CRITIQUE OF
THE IDEA OF THE GOOD

But how, then, do things look with regard to Aristotle's critique of the good? Is there still any real object for his criticism? And what about his critique of the doctrine of the ideas? Let this last question be our guide, and let us scrutinize Aristotle's critique in light of the insights we have gained in our study of Plato. On methodological grounds, let us leave aside the reconstruction of no longer extant texts—in Plato's case, the reconstruction of his forbidding lecture "On the Good." Instead, let us confine ourselves to the three ethical treatises found in the corpus of Aristotle's works. As far as these are concerned, we do not even need to involve ourselves in the question whether all three are authentic. Especially after Dirlmeier's commentaries on the *Magna Moralia* and the *Eudemian Ethics*,[1] it may be considered certain that we are dealing here in any case with an authentic legacy of Aristotelian thought: the concordance of these three texts in their three critiques of Plato is almost overwhelming.[2] And cer-

1. F. Dirlmeier, translations of, and commentaries on, Aristotle's *Ethica Nicomachia* (Darmstadt, 1956), *Magna Moralia* (Darmstadt, 1958), and *Ethica Eudemia* (Berlin, 1962).

2. Recently, the strikingly didactic style of *MM* has been brought to the fore by Brink, Theiler, and Dirlmeier, and rightly so. It seems to me that the simplest hypothesis here—a hypothesis that also accounts for certain stylistic peculiarities and obscurities in the composition of the work—is still that we are dealing with

tainly the texts themselves dictate our general methodological principle: namely, to bring things in common to the fore, to emphasize these things in common over the differences, and to use each text to elucidate the other two. Moreover, our principle enjoins us not to concern ourselves with attempts to ascribe individual arguments to specific "Platonists" (cf. the research of Arnim, Gigon, and others). For again, the truly significant thing is not so much the divergence of these arguments from one another but the common character of the argumentation that persists throughout all variation and that all three of Aristotle's critiques evince. In individual cases it may well be debatable whether everything that is weighed and subjected to critical refutation in them is actually founded on Plato's own teachings, or whether some of it derives from later speculative elaborations of these teachings. But since Aristotle does not seek to give a reliable account anyway, and since his critical aims as such must always be taken into consideration—as the works of Cherniss, more than any others, have convincingly demonstrated—our approach can only be to evaluate Aristotle's assertions starting with the set of problems implied by the subject matter in Plato himself, that is, to evaluate Aristotle's assertions from the perspective of those problems. For our purposes we need not concern ourselves with the question of just who it might have been who developed the individual arguments.[3]

---

some sort of copy by someone else, that is, not with the text of the "author," but with carefully reworked class notes. In particular, the "logical concern" of the text, of which Dirlmeier correctly takes note, can be easily explained as a consequence of the lecture's skeletal treatment of its topic. And many "deviations" in the line of thought in *MM* [from *EE* and *EN*], for example, the delayed introduction of *eudaimonia*, would not be all that surprising if we are dealing with a rendering of a live lecture which was not intended as a text to be read.

3. Is *MM* 1182a25 ff. an allusion to the lost lecture on the good or, rather, a polemic against the *Republic*? Can *apedōken hekastōi* (assigned to each [part of

Also, let us keep away from any hypothesis about the relationship of these three ethical treatises to each other. We find the critique of the idea of the good at the beginning of all three, and in
all three that critique is aimed precisely at the universal ontological claim which Plato makes *for his idea of the good*. In all
three the decisive argument is that knowledge of such a good can
have no relevance for the philosophy of human practice. In the
Magna Moralia (1182a25 ff.) Plato is criticized precisely for having introduced the question of aretē (virtue) at all into his universal ontological doctrine of the agathon (the good)—as he did in
his famous lecture "On the Good." According to this argument,
for Aristotle, the Socratic question about aretē would be wholly
incompatible with the universal question of the good, to which
Platonic dialectic is addressed. Here Aristotle in fact raises the
very same question that we put to the text of the *Republic*,
*namely, how the Socratic question about the good and the as-
cent to dialectic through and past the mathematical sciences relate
to each other. In what follows I intend to show that Aristotle, the
creator of physics and founder of practical philosophy, holds
fast to the Socratic heritage in Plato: the good is the practically
good. On the other hand, as the creator of physics, Aristotle also
fulfills the demand made by Plato's Socrates, that is, that we understand the world starting with the experience of the good. The
good thus appears in Aristotle's physics as well as his practical

---

the soul]) be anything other than an allusion to book 4 of the *Republic*? Above
all, the phrase at 1182a27, *kai synezeuxen* (and coupled [aretē and the good]),
speaks for such an understanding of the allusion. In substance the critical observation would then amount to a rejection of Plato's having extended the so-called
four-book *Republic*. Or perhaps one must read the note as follows: Plato's lecture on the good would have been just fine had he only omitted all references to
the aretai. That would fit well with the account of Aristoxenus. To be sure, I am
of the opinion that in this case no one other than Aristotle himself said this, and
that he was attempting to reverse popular expectations with such sarcasm.

philosophy—in his physics as the hou heneka, in his practical philosophy as the *anthrōpinon agathon*. This double function of the good can be demonstrated using the text of his critiques of the idea of the good. Thus one sees that his philosophy of human practice remains embedded in the whole of his conceptualization of reality.*

Aristotle's restriction of his inquiry to the concerns of practical philosophy does not silence the question of just what constitutes the common property in all being-good. For it is surely not just a superficial equivocation that such a diversity of things are called good. What the *Nichomachean Ethics* states expressly— *ou gar eoike [to agathon] tois ge apo tychēs homōnumois* ([the good] is indeed not like those things that only have the same name by chance) (1096b26)—holds all the more for the other two treatises. The *Magna Moralia* comes close to granting the argument that what is most good, *to malista agathon*, the good itself, must be an idea, which is to say, the good of all ideas: *alēthēs men estin isōs . . .* (that is perhaps true . . .) (1183a32). And the mutilated closing sentence of the critique in the *Eudemian Ethics* virtually seems to demand the investigation of the multiple meanings of agathon with an eye to the ariston pantōn (the best of all things), once the ariston tōn praktōn (the best of the practical) has been treated (1218a25).⁴ In any case, the author of

4. To be sure, in emending the text Dirlmeier attempts to eliminate the *posachōs* (in how many senses ["best of all" is said]) and, with that, the allusion to the universal problem of the good. But in regard to 1218b4 ff., which in its content is close to 1217a31 ff., I find that unacceptable. In these passages either agatha (goods) or a part of the agathon are mentioned, which are not prakton. Of course I do not know if Aristotle himself wrote *skepteon posachōs* (it remains to be investigated in how many ways . . .] in this spot after the concluding statement, which, together with the addition in question reads: "*to d' hōs telos agathon anthrōpōi (esti) kai to ariston tōn praktōn, skepteon posachōs to ariston pantōn*" (the good for human beings [exists] as the goal and the best of prac-

the *Eudemian Ethics* also has the broad sense of a comprehensive agathon very much in mind. Thus we can establish that in all three treatises Aristotle does not limit himself to what for him is the decisive argument concerning the practical relevance of the idea of the good. Instead, he finds himself forced beyond the confines of his theme of practice.[5]

---

tices—it remains to be investigated in how many ways "the best of all" [applies]). The last part *could* have been appended by an editor who wished, after this summary, to remind us of the larger universal ontological horizons here. But in any case, in our text (1218a25 ff.), the contrast between to ariston tōn praktōn (the best of practices) and to ariston pantōn (the best of all) is manifest.

Here, a general observation concerning the status of our texts is in order. Gigon likes to speak of an editor but leaves open the question of whether this editor was Aristotle himself. He is entirely right insofar as one may not always apply the yardstick of stylistic consistency appropriate to a literary exposition of doctrine—even to the ethical treatises. But his predicates (negligent, careless, imprecise, and so forth) go too far. One should not allow oneself to be deceived in such fashion that one mistakes single locutions, often subtly and cleverly formulated, for a text. To be specific: the composition is indeed often "careless," or better said, dependent on the kind of care that would be given to it in oral presentation.

5. Things like this occur elsewhere in Aristotle. For example, his definition of physics ought, strictly speaking, to prohibit any discussion of Eleatic philosophy whatsoever within the framework of physics, for Eleatic philosophy, after all, denies the existence of motion altogether. Nevertheless, he inserts his critique of the Eleatics in his lectures on physics (Alpha 3, 4). In the case we are considering the definition of practical philosophy ought, strictly speaking, to preclude a detailed discussion of Plato's idea of the good. Nonetheless, he takes it up, even if he constantly points out that it actually belongs in another context. It would seem that he is somehow uncertain of just where to find an appropriate place for such things. Ultimately one must say, then, that such uncertainties, which often occur in Aristotle, reflect the larger uncertainty we call "metaphysics." The stack of papers that later received this name is, so to speak, a collection of uncertainties that share this character of being marginal. Once one is clear about this fact, it is no longer very puzzling that the start made in Book Gamma, which gives the impression that the science to be pursued is a formal ontology, does not quite fit with what is begun in Books Zeta and Eta (the doctrine of substance and of dynamis and *energeia*) and in Book Lambda (the so-called theology), and that the book of aporiai, Beta, stands by itself in a peculiar way. The fact that Book Epsilon ultimately provides a certain editorial harmonization of what precedes it, does not contradict what I have said here.

The category argument thus finds a place in all three treatises. Of course, it is particularly well suited to repudiate the claim that a universal science of the good is relevant practically. But at the same time its very usefulness here suggests that the problem of the good remains indissolubly tied to the problem of being. In regard to being, there is a genuine question how the various senses of the word, that of "substance" and those of the other categories, are related to one another. And the same would seem to hold necessarily for being-good. As a matter of fact, in regard to both being and the good, Aristotle directs us to the problem of analogy (*analogia*). So he is not at all blind to the universal ontological question of the good, despite his critique of Plato in the three ethical treatises. It is only the practical concern that prevails in his ethics that allows him to dodge the problem in a facile way, but—and this is the point—not completely.

Aristotle takes up Plato's doctrine and the refutation of it most extensively in the *Eudemian Ethics*. Hence it serves our purposes to fix our sights on that work, not, of course, without bringing in both the other treatises as well for clarification. Let the results of our study of Plato be our guide here. It emerged there that in Plato too, "knowledge of the good" was a special kind of knowing "beyond" the "sciences," a mode of knowing that had a different epistemological structure from technē. Unlike the latter, it does not attempt to draw inferences from given presuppositions but consists, instead, in giving justification (*logon didonai*) of the highest *telos* (goal or purpose), that is, justification in the sense of dialectical exploration and elucidation of what Hegel calls the "concrete universal." Do we not find the good in everything outside of human praxis (practice), as well as in what is prakton (of practical concern)? Is it not the immanent measure (the *metrion* of the *Statesman*) in the soul, the state, and the world? And precisely in regard to the idea of the good, is not talk of the chōrismos (separation) especially misleading?

We can expect that the critical purposes for which Aristotle wrote his ethics will prevent this way of seeing things from surfacing by itself. The opposite clearly holds: he must play down the "transcendence of the good," which, if he did not, would set it apart from all ideas. He must put the idea of the good in the same class as the other ideas. Consequently, he must be particularly emphatic in insisting that *like other ideas* the idea of the good exists for itself separately (*chōriston*).

*One must keep in mind that the concept chōriston has two aspects in Plato and Aristotle. On the one hand, it refers to a thing's being separate and, on the other, to its consisting in itself (*In-sich-stehen*). If one starts with the latter, Aristotle's ontological deviation from Plato becomes understandable at once. It is not the ideas that consist in themselves but rather the *physei onta* (things which are by nature), and, ultimately, the highest existent thing, the god. For Plato it is precisely these things that do not exist for themselves, but rather, only the ideas. The divine—like the good—is beyond being (*epekeina tēs ousias*), in a sense that prohibits its being called an existent thing. For Plato, eidetic or noetic constructs, for example, numbers, lines, and so forth, are to be separated from phenomenal existence, not fused with it as the Pythagoreans held. For Aristotle, the physei onta are inseparable from their ti estin (what-it-is). That is the meaning of his doctrine of primary and secondary substance (*ousia*). But that means, conversely, that the eidos is not to be separated from its phenomenal appearance and, thus, that it is an *enhylon eidos* (materialized form). And to this extent not only the todi ti (this-whatever), but also the ti (what) is "separate" from all other *symbebēkota* (accidents). That, too, is a fundamental departure from Plato. What methexis is in Plato—a being together [*koinōnia* (coupling)] of ideas, for example, of human being and whiteness—is in Aristotle predication that refers to a subject,

the *synholon* (underlying whole). Still, the question remains: despite these differences,* is it not possible that what Plato truly intended becomes visible in Aristotle's discussion, nevertheless—
against the latter's will, as it were?[6]

6. Gadamer grants that this chapter in particular often needs to be filled out.
The argument as stated here, for instance, is somewhat compressed. As I understand it, the line of thought that Gadamer is pursuing is as follows: Aristotle
wishes to include the idea of the good in his general critique of the ideas, which
argues that Plato unnecessarily doubles the world by postulating that the ideas
have a chōriston reality apart from the things that they inform. For Aristotle, being chōriston is indeed a characteristic of anything that is; for anything that is,
exists for itself and in itself, which is to say, exists as "what it is" (*ti estin*) apart
from changing accidental predications (the *katēgoroumena* or symbebēkota). A
horse is a horse in itself, apart from (*chōriston*) being brown or old, here or there,
next to this or smaller than that. But, according to Aristotle, Plato is guilty of a
misplaced concretion, so to speak, insofar as he assigns precisely this being chōriston to the ideas themselves, as if they too were realities, while in fact only a this-
something (*tode ti*) is real and chōriston. When Aristotle comes to the idea of the
good in Plato, he finds the same mistake that Plato makes with all the ideas:
Plato, he says, treats the good as if it were a thing in itself, and that leads to an
empty abstraction: "We say first, then, that to say there is an idea not only of the
good, but of anything else whatever, is to say something abstract and empty"
(*EE* 1217b20).
    This criticism, of course, accords with Aristotle's overall project, but it must
systematically suppress the fact that Plato himself argues that the good transcends all existence, that is, that it is epekeina tēs ousias. As Gadamer has shown,
despite all the differences, Plato's aim is to make just Aristotle's point: the idea of
the good is precisely not another thing alongside things that are good; rather, it is
the structural order in any thing that is good. We call the good, insofar as it exists, the beautiful—a shining forth in things, an appearance. Aristotle's intended
criticism thus actually reinforces Plato's point.
    One should not overlook the fact that, for the purposes of his critique, Aris-
totle shifts the weight of chōriston ever so slightly. As Gadamer has shown
above, chōriston in Plato implied independence from contingencies, as circularity
is independent of the aberrations that may occur in any particular circles we may
draw (see "Dialectic and Sophism in Plato's *Seventh Letter*"). Aristotle, too,
would not deny that what a thing is in essence is separate, or distinct, from the
variable things that might be said of it.
    But since his starting point is the living thing (*tode ti*), not mathematics, he also

In interpreting the idea of the good, the *Eudemian Ethics*, Alpha 8, begins with two interpretive formulations of the idea of the good, which, in tying into Plato's assertions, are as faithful to him as one could possibly imagine. The first states that the good is that which is first (*prōton*), the negation (*anhairein*) of which also negates everything else (*to heteron*) that follows from what is first and is therefore "good" *just as when there is no longer such a thing as line, for instance, there can no longer be a triangle composed of lines*. Although it does not occur in the dialogues themselves, this formulation has an undeniably Platonic stamp, as P. Wilpert, in particular, has demonstrated.[7] Konrad Gaiser, whose argument we touched on above, has convincingly shown that the system of the mathematical disciplines is a sequential order of number, point, line, plane, and solid, and he takes this mathematical system to be a kind of schema for Plato's overall systematization. It is obvious that the numbers stand or

---

takes chōriston to mean "unto itself" in the way that a thing exists self-identically apart from other things. Thus the *chōra* (space) in *chōriston* is much more present in Aristotle's understanding of the word, albeit in a transfigured sense. As a "physical" thinker, Aristotle has an ear for this *chōra*, or "spatial" separation, of whatever is chōriston.

Now if, like Aristotle, one starts with this sense of *chōriston* and then applies the word to the ideas, it does indeed appear that there is a misplaced concretion—almost as if the ideas were said to be things "spatially" apart from the things that participate in them, and hence Aristotle's argument that Plato needlessly doubles the world. Gadamer's point, however, is that thinking of the ideas as chōriston in this sense is obviously every bit as much of a mistake in Plato's eyes too; in fact, it is precisely the mistake in which the young Socrates gets caught in all his attempts to defend the ideas in the *Parmenides*. There can be no doubt that Aristotle knew this. Hence we can only assume that he consciously slants Plato's thought in order to better articulate his own "physicalist" position; in fact, he marshals Plato's very own arguments—again consciously—to attack the chōriston idea (for example, the "third man"). TRANSLATOR.

7. P. Wilpert, *Zwei aristotelische Frühschriften über die Ideenlehre* (Regensburg, 1949).

fall with the one—and, of course, with the two as well. In our text too, something follows that concurs with this line of argument. Aristotle says (*EE* 1218a15 ff.) that we may not deduce the good from the numbers but instead from what everybody acknowledges to be good. Conversely, at the very most, we can conclude from the being-good of types of order in things (such as health or harmony of the soul) that the numbers too, on account of their ordered structure, are good in a certain sense. The numbers are then described as "striving" toward the one—a metaphor that Aristotle in his accustomed manner, takes literally (*EE* 1218a22 ff.).[8] Here too, given my purposes, the concern is not to establish whether this doctrine is the special teaching of some Platonist. Even if it were, it would still be a conclusion drawn from Plato's doctrine of the good and the one, a conclusion that, in the context of our investigation, has to be of interest to us. The principle of the *prōton*, which the *Eudemian Ethics* takes as its point of departure, is in any case palpable in the numbers. At this point a question forces itself upon us: if the numbers have the central function suggested here, how, exactly, do things stand with regard to the *chōrismos* of the good? And how do things stand with regard to the *chōrismos* of the ideas if the ideas are numbers? After all, are not the numbers *in* the things? (Again I refer the reader to the *Philebus* 16d.) And is not the one, which resides in all numbers, each being a manifold of ones, actually "separated from itself" while in them? If one interprets the ideas

---

8. Instead of *agathon*, Aristotle says *kalon* here (cf. *Metaphysics* 1078a31 ff.). But surely he does so solely to reserve *agathon* here for what is *prakton* and to avoid misunderstandings. This, it seems to me, is a minimal terminological differentiation, which Aristotle makes for his own purposes, a modification that accords with the close concatenation of *agathon* and *kalon* in Plato's language usage. Hence I would not ground any hypothesis concerning divergent teachings on the passages bearing on this one that Dirlmeier carefully assembles, and certainly not any hypothesis concerning Aristotle's "development."

as numbers, this puzzling and deliberately contradictory formulation of Plato's (cf. *Philebus* 15b: *autēn hautēs chōris*, and *Parmenides* 131b) becomes understandable at once: the one-ness of the one is both *for itself* and *in* the numbers.

That brings us to the second formulation, which may count as good Plato if anything may, and which is solidly documented precisely in reference to the idea of the good as well as the other ideas. It is the general formulation for "participation" (*methexis*), which is also used elsewhere in Plato in speaking of participation in the ideas. Here it is applied to the good, whose presence (*parousia*) is said to cause all things that are good to be good (*EE* 1217b5). Precisely this formulation is used to introduce the idea of the good in the *Republic* (book 6, 505a). That the good is the most important subject matter (*megiston mathēma*) because it embraces everything is advanced as a kind of self-evident argument. It will be recalled, of course, that presence (*parousia*), participation (*methexis*), and similarity (*homiotēs*)[9] are always only metaphors, which the young Socrates of the *Parmenides* cannot succeed in conceptualizing when the old Parmenides locks him in his Socratic grip. If one wishes to understand the aims and limits of Aristotle's critique of Plato, one must constantly keep this fact in mind. Aristotle must have been aware of it when he repeated the very argument here that, as Plato himself had shown in the *Parmenides*, leads to an insoluble problem (*aporia*) and an absurdity, that is, the complete separation of the ideas from the appearances.

As I have shown, indications of a substantive answer to the question of what is there, what is present, when something is

---

9. *Homiotēs*, incidentally, is the preferred expression in Diogenes Laertius's account of Alcimus, whose ties with the old academy Gaiser has argued for convincingly (*Rheinisches Museum für Philologie*, Frankfurt, 1975).

"good," are most likely to be had if, in some vague way, we take the triad of *metron, symmetron,* and *alēthes* (measured, symmetrical, and true) that constitutes the beautiful in the *Philebus,* to be what is first (*prōton*) and gives oneness to things. In any case, the structure of Plato's *Republic* also implies that somehow the good is the one: the "oneness" of the ideal city is a unified order of such a nature that neither strife nor disturbance can occur in it. That the good is what is first and gives oneness to things is also implied, incidentally, in Aristotle's critique in the *Nicomachean Ethics.* Aristotle's express praise there of the Pythagoreans for simply putting the one in the series of good things and consequently, unlike Plato, not equating the one with the good (*EN* 1096b5), obviously presupposes that for his part Plato did think of the good as the one. Of course, Plato's one is not at all a Neoplatonic *hen* (One). On the contrary, in the *Parmenides* insoluble puzzles are displayed in the concepts of being and oneness in order to establish the dialectical unity of the one and the many.[10]

In returning to Aristotle's introduction of his Plato critique in the *Eudemian Ethics,* which we discussed above, we can now see that there Aristotle is striving for the least metaphorical exposition possible of what is meant by the idea of the good. Being primary among all those things that are good and being the cause of everything other than itself by virtue of its presence—these are obviously two aspects of Plato's methexis metaphor. First, as the

---

10. The critique in the *Metaphysics,* Alpha 6, introduces Plato as a Pythagorean and works him into the doctrine of the archē in the same way as in other places in the first book of the *Metaphysics.* In contrast, Alpha 9 exceeds this framework and, for its part, fits perfectly in the arrangement of the doublet of this passage in Mu: *aisthēta mathematikē-megethē-ideai-arithmoi* (perceptible-mathematical-magnitude-ideas-numbers). How the two chapters fit together, and how the chōrismos critique in Alpha 9 is materially connected with the archē doctrine in Alpha 6 are, of course, not explained by this observation.

principle of number, the good is primary logically. That, as we saw, is a genuinely Platonic line of argument, which Aristotle often mentions under the heading of the logical term *synanhairein* (suspension or negation of the species by suspension of the genus) (cf. *Topics* 141b28; *Metaphysics* 1059b30 and elsewhere). Second, the good is the highest presence (eminently good) and, precisely for that reason, the cause of everything good being good—via participation. It is striking that Aristotle, in dealing with this second aspect [of Plato's *methexis* metaphor], only pursues the *chōrismos* argument incidentally, an argument which, given Plato's *Parmenides* with its decisive repudiation of the chōrismos, is not without problems of its own.[11] That is to say, he places the idea of the good in parallel with the other ideas *insofar as both are said to be "separate" (*chōriston*)*. Aristotle evidently senses full well that the good, which is the object of his concern here, does not quite fit among the ideas taken as the genera of species. (Ultimately, this disparity also holds for being itself, and it will be recalled that the highest determinations supervening upon being in the *Sophist* are only called "species" of it in an improper sense.) Hence Aristotle does say of the idea of the good: "*kai gar chōristēn einai . . . hōsper kai tas allas ideas*" (and it is indeed separate for itself . . . like the other ideas) (*EE* 1217b15). But that is a questionable argument. After all, Plato singled out the good as above the level of realities (*epekeina tēs ousias*). Aristotle deliberately ignores that here and is emphatic

---

11. It might be recalled that the *Parmenides*—which constitutes a sort of conerstone in my argument—does not stand by itself. The *Sophist, Philebus,* and the *Statesman* attach so little value to the chōrismos of the ideas that some people, in fact, have even attempted to find in them a turning away from the doctrine of ideas. Of course, that creates difficulties in regard to both the *Philebus* and the *Timaeus,* and above all it makes the enigma of Aristotle's critique of the ideas that much more impenetrable.

in equating the idea of the good with the general postulation of the ideas. Clearly, he wants the full weight of his critique of the ideas, to which he refers here, to fall on Plato's idea of the good (cf. 1217b20: "... to einai idean mē monon agathou alla kai allou otououn" ([it is empty to assert] that there is an idea, not only of the good, but also of anything else whatever).

Then he introduces his second and, he says, decisive argument: the idea of the good is useless in practice. It is striking that this argument is later treated only very briefly (1218b34). In introducing it, he inadvertently lets a peculiarly clumsy sentence go by: "ei kai hoti malist' eisin hai ideai kai agathou idea ..." (And however much there are ideas and an idea of the good [they are perhaps useless in regard to a good life and to practice]) (1217b23).

To be sure, the general, logical argument against the doctrine of the ideas as a whole is not repeated in what follows. But it is remarkable that the particular question of the idea of the good, which is taken up now, is pursued exclusively along the paths of logic. One must ask oneself if the kinds of argument used here do not actually, if unintentionally, confirm the special status of the idea of the good. For Aristotle does not simply bring the chōrismos critique to bear on the idea of the good and let it go at that. Rather, independent arguments are devoted to the question, arguments designed to display the contradictoriness of the idea of the good (1218b33).

To begin with, we find the category argument, which places the good in strict parallel with being: "oude to on hen ti esti peri ta eirēmena ..." (being is not one thing in all that we have spoken of [and neither is the good]) (1217b33). This argument, of course, precludes any being-for-itself (chōriston) of the idea of the good. But does it not go too far? For it would follow from this parallel [not only] that no science [is possible for the good, but also that none] is possible for being as such (1217b34). Obviously, the *Nicomachean Ethics*, as well as the *Magna Moralia*, seeks to avoid this undesired consequence. Hence, when the *Nicomachean Ethics* uses the same argument, it speaks only of the good and rules out that it could be "something universal and one" (*koinon ti katholou kai hen*) (*EN* 1096a28). In general, it is striking that in the *Nicomachean Ethics* "being-chōriston" is mentioned only once and is used primarily as a synonym for "*koinēi kategoroumenon*" (predicable in common) (1096b32 ff.). Here the issue is the *koinos logos* (common expression).

The kind of argument that follows next is taken from the sciences and based on the category argument. According to it, knowledge of the good disappears among the particular arts (*technai*). Actually, Aristotle thereby touches on the same, familiar difficulty which we uncovered in Plato, that is, the difficulty which arises when one tries to understand the good taking the mode of knowing in the arts as a starting point. To be sure, Aristotle's rejection of a science of the good is meant as a criticism of Plato—*scholēi auto ge to agathon theōresai mias* (there can hardly be a sole theorizing about the good itself) (*EE* 1218a1) or *ēn an mia tis epistēmē* there would have to be [but cannot be] a single science) (*EN* 1096a30). But in Plato's dialogues too, equating knowledge of the good with the mode of knowing in the arts tended to miscarry. Accordingly, Aristotle does not seem so far removed from what Plato had in mind even when he criticizes him.

There is a difficulty with the second argument (*EE* 1218a1–15). The text of the *Eudemian Ethics* cannot be right here. The point is that the good cannot be both something in common and something for itself (*koinon kai chōriston*). But it seems to me that the line of thought here is incoherent and cannot be followed out to a logical conclusion. The *prōteron-hysteron* (prior-subsequent) argument and the illustration of it with the numbers is familiar to us from the *Nicomachean Ethics*. That there are no ideas of the numbers because there could be no idea of number as such is specifically cited there as a Platonic doctrine. And there, Aristotle uses Plato's own reasoning in arguing against the idea of the good. In view of the privileged position of substance over the other categories, which are only subsequent to it, the good, just like the numbers, would have to be excepted from the postulation of an idea. That is: if the number per se were what is first (*to prōton*), the first number would no longer be the first number, and that argument ought to hold analogously for the good per se.

The exposition in the *Eudemian Ethics* of the same argument that led Plato to reject the postulation of an idea of number for the numbers is entirely accurate: the "multiple" can only be something in common and not something existing for itself. Hence, there is no idea here. This was obviously the conclusion Plato drew. But how does Aristotle then proceed to derive an argument against the idea of the good from Plato's own teaching? The text does not say explicitly. We must, it would seem, assume (as in *EE* 1218a15 and a24) that the good is thought of here as the one, that is, as the first in the series of the ideal numbers.[12] Then the argument makes sense, and only then is there no

12. Thus 1218a6: "If, for example, duality is the first in the series of the multiple, the concept common (to all multiples), 'multiplicity,' cannot be separable. For if what is in common is the idea—if, that is, one were to make 'the common' separate (*chōriston*)—multiplicity would be prior to duality."

The point is that multiplicity (*pollaplasion*) is a principle *in* number and not another numerical entity. Two, as Gadamer will point out, is the first arithmos, since arithmos or number, is by definition *sum* number. Hence there are two principles in number: the one, or unity of so and so many (which unity is precisely not a number), and multiplicity. Any arithmos is a unity of many. Compare "Plato's Unwritten Dialectic." TRANSLATOR.

need of a detour by way of the categories. Just as there is no idea
of the numbers, so too there is no idea of the good for itself. The
one of the ideal numbers cannot be an "idea existing for itself" if
it is the first number of a series. That is Aristotle's objection.

But how does the argument, augmented in this way, relate to
what follows? How does it relate to what is common (*koinon*) to
all virtues? Certainly the issue continues to be whether a universal is to be viewed as something existing for itself. And in some
form or other, something like this question is in fact raised in the
corrupted traditional text: "*ei chōriston poiēseie tis to koinon*"
(if one were to make that which is in common separate and for
itself) (*EE* 1218a9). That is a conditional charged with skepti-
cism. Nonetheless, it introduces an entirely new argument,
namely, the hypostasizing of the good as the thing common to all
virtues. Pure induction leads from dikaiosynē (justice) and
andreia (courage) to a common being-good. We find that argument in the *Magna Moralia* at 1182b31—as the *kat' epagōgen
koinon* (thing in common arrived at by induction)—and its logical structure is clear. To start with, the good is nothing other
than the common logos (expression) and now the Platonists pro-

---

The argument with the numbers, then, extends the general "third man" argument against any chōriston idea, and in particular, the idea of the good (see n. 6
above). It is a misplaced concretion to turn the principle of something into another thing like the thing of which it is the principle, and thereby make it part of
the same series of things. That will only necessitate yet another principle governing the new series—ad infinitum.

It now becomes clear why Gadamer treated Plato's *hōsautōs* in the *Republic* so
extensively (cf. ch. 3 above). If Gadamer is right, Plato could not have meant
hōsautōs in a way that would lead to a strict equation of the good with the other
ideas. For, as the one is a principle of number and not a number itself, so too, the
idea of the good is the principle of the ideas and not an idea itself. (It will be
noted, of course, that here we are moving within eidetic realm and not as before,
between the eidetic and phenomenal realms. Even so, the structure of Aristotle's
argument remains the same.) TRANSLATOR.

ceed to call it "itself" (*auto*), by which they must mean "eternal" (*aidion*) and "for itself" (*chōriston*). This line of thought appears to end in a conclusion which Aristotle draws: if it is "itself," then it is "for itself," and in that case it is not something "in common." For what is in common is an attribute not of a particular individual thing but of all individual things (*EE* 1218a15 = *MM* 1182b13). Now if one considers all those things that argued for the fact that Plato himself also had in mind no other presence of the good than its presence in all good things, the deduction of its being for itself (*chōriston*) from its being eternal (*aidion*) is, to say the very least, quite misleading. This deduction is more an expression of what in Aristotle's view is an unavoidable consequence than of what Plato intended.[13]

It seems to me that something similar holds in regard to what follows. Aristotle now criticizes Plato's inference from the numbers, for the being-good (being-beautiful) of the numbers can perhaps be deduced from those things that are accepted as good, for example, justice and health, and the ordered structure that pertains to these, but not vice versa. Let us forget the aims of Aristotle's critique for a moment and consider the Platonic argument per se, that the good is found in orders of things and in numbers. But is it separate from them? Is the unity of an order of things separate from the order itself? It makes no sense to say that it is. In the mythology of the *Timaeus* too, the world soul, to which the order of the motion of the universe conforms, is spoken of as a harmony composed of pure ratios. But the one is not spoken of as the good. In our passage (1218a30), to be sure, we have "the striving of all numbers for the one," *as if it were a

---

13. Perhaps the addition that Rassow and Susemihl insert at 1218a 14 is unnecessary, since Aristotelian explications of the meanings of *auto, aidion,* and *chōriston* constitute a unity, and the argument is intended to show only the incompatibility of these with whatever is *koinon.*

good*. That, however, is just a metaphor, and Aristotle, in his familiar fashion, makes things easy for himself when he takes this metaphor of the striving of the numbers literally and then finds that the numbers ought to have soul(s) but do not. Just what, however, does the metaphor actually stand for? Does it really stand for the being-for-itself of the one?

The numbers are units of ones. The principle of being one is generative in them. They all follow the principle of $n + 1$. That they do is obviously the sole meaning of the being of the number one, just as the sole meaning of the one *or unit* of the world order is being that one order. Plato is able to express this fact only in such fashion that it looks as if the world were striving to come as close as possible to the pure numerical relationships, and as if, for their part, the pure numbers and measures that constitute the order of the universe were being "striven for." Evidently, the ideal order in the *Timaeus* is called "world soul" on account of this movement toward the pure numbers and measures. When it is said that not only all numbers, but all existences, strive for the one and the good, that is to be taken in this metaphorical sense. But surely Plato would not find Aristotle's objection that every individual thing strives for its own good, for its measure (*EE* 1218a31), an objection. In the mythical language of the *Timaeus*, this same idea is expressed when it is said that the self-moved heavenly bodies follow a course prescribed for them ("*to prostachthen emathen*" [they learned what had been commanded]) (*Timaeus* 36e). And what does Socrates do in the *Philebus* but raise precisely this issue [of each thing's striving for its own good]? But whereas all other living things strive for their proper good instinctively, human beings are special insofar as they choose theirs, using reason.

To this extent, the difficulty that Aristotle creates by deliberately taking Plato literally is an artificial one: the dialectical perplexities (*aporiai*) (1218a33) are contrived. They are designed to introduce Aristotle's own solution: there can be no "good itself," no "good in itself," except in the functional sense of the telos (goal) or hou heneka (that for the sake of which). This conclusion emerges at 1218b20. His arguments are based on a literal reading of Plato's metaphorical statements within the framework of his own conceptual apparatus. But for just that reason they miss what Plato intended.

Thus the actual question before us is as follows. If the idea of the good is "the good itself," it must be common to all things that are good. But what does that mean? In the end, does it not mean that "it itself" is nothing other than what is common to all things? Such an interpretation of the doctrine of the idea of the good—namely, that it means nothing except the *koinon* (what is in common)—might have been advocated by liberal Platonists, for instance, and might even accord with what Plato himself intended. But whether it does or not has no bearing whatever on Aristotle's argument. The important thing for us is that, whatever the case, for Aristotle, too, the question of just what it is that is in common remains inescapable. The inevitability of this question is also confirmed by the fact that he gives his own positive answer to it—*to telos tōn anthrōpōi praktōn* (the goal of human actions) (1218b)—while expressly mentioning the *ou prakta* (what is non-practical), and in fact even the *akinēta* (what is unmoved) *in order to exclude them from consideration: "Moreover the good is spoken of in many ways, some of which are the noble and practical, as well as the nonpractical. The practical good, however, is that for the sake of which. It is not something in the realm of what is unmoved" (1218b4 ff.)*.[14] Hence

14. The reference here is to the stars, which, it will be noted, the Pythagoreans called "good." TRANSLATOR.

the foundations of ethics are provided by a kind of narrowing of the question about the good to the prakton (practical). Within the range of "practical" problems, the question of what is good and, at the same time, one and unifying is easily answered, and in all three treatises it receives the same answer: "that for the sake of which" (*to hou heneka*). In each case the for-the-sake-of-which is the good, and it comprehends within itself that which contributes to this end, which is to say, the means [to achieve it]. But clearly the best in human action is something different in each case, that is, not something common to all cases, and least of all, common to all existent things in general. The concern here is solely with the ariston tōn praktōn (the best of actions). But as clear as that is, the question of how such a "practical" best relates to the "best of all things" remains meaningful. And, as a matter of fact, the text that concludes the critique of Plato in the *Eudemian Ethics* raises a question aimed in this direction: *skepteon, posachōs to ariston pantōn* (it remains to examine the best of all things in general) (1218b26). I have treated the corrupted text above (see n. 4), and I hope that my analysis of the context of Aristotle's argument has demonstrated convincingly that the phrase "posachōs to ariston pantōn" cannot be conjured out of existence. It corresponds to the *pollachōs* (in many ways) at 1218b4. The question is prepared for there—a question that is most likely raised in our passage with the sole intent of showing that the practical good, although it only has to do with a narrower realm, can also be called a "best of all." That Aristotle says this, however, in no way alters the fact that the more general question is found in the text here as an unelaborated question mark.

Fortunately we do not have to depend exclusively on the unreliable text of the *Eudemian Ethics*. Both the other treatises confirm that an outlook [as it were] into the universal is always nearby. To begin with, let us turn to the *Magna Moralia*. The first thing that strikes us is that the argument starts out with the question of aretē. But then it proceeds to the question of the agathon, and it is clear that with this transition Plato's line of questioning is taken up. Of course, right away his question is restricted to the "good for us," the single and highest object of "politics." Still, it should be noted that the concept of the agathon and the multiplicity of its meanings continue to be the general, guiding theme. That may be the reason why the expression for the restricted topic characteristic of the *Eudemian Ethics* and the *Nicomachean Ethics*, namely, *prakton agathon*, never occurs at all in the *Magna Moralia*. So one must ask oneself just what the restriction here to the "good for us" actually signifies. It is introduced in vague distinction to the "good for the god," which brings no universal ontological or teleological implications to mind. Then, still another distinction is introduced within this reduced "good for us": "*palin de kai touto dielein dei*" (moreover, we ought to distinguish in this too) (1182b6). The distinction needed, we are told, is between the two meanings of "good" here: on the one hand, to be good in the general sense (called here "*to koinon*" [what is in common]), and on the other, to be the "idea of the good." These are two renderings of "good." The first refers to a being-in-the-individual, the second to that in which the individual participates: "*ē to ariston en hekastōi tōn ontōn ē hou talla metaschonta*" (either the best in each existent thing or that of which another partakes) (1182b8). The consideration of both senses would seem to have its locus within the framework of politics, that is, of the "good for us," but, at least when Aristotle takes up the doctrine of the ideas, this framework is broken through. "The good" in *both* these senses is rejected as untenable.

Even in the *Eudemian Ethics* we do not find these alternatives in the interpretation of the good. There, being-for-itself is always explicitly associated with "what is in common." Here, in the *Magna Moralia*, on the other hand, the good of each individual, as the *koinon en hapasin hyparchon* (the common thing occurring in each (*MM* 1182b11), is divorced in an illuminating way from the being-for-itself (*chōriston kai auto kath' hauto* [separate and itself for itself]) (1182b13) that the idea of the good presupposes: the good as the koinon has only the logical universality of a genus. It is treated in regard to each of the two possibilities of arriving at a universal—definition and induction—and is rejected on the grounds that it can be established as a universal in neither of these ways. Obviously the good, which is discussed here as the "universal" (*koinon*)—at 1182b20 the same thing is called *katholou*—and whose definition is what is *auto di' hauto haireton* (to be chosen for its own sake), is thematized entirely within the context of politics and is to be understood accordingly, that is, as the good for us. (We know this definition from Plato's *Republic*, book 2 [357b] and from the detailed critique of the *idea* at *EN* 1096b16, where the good is taken to be the one consideration [*mia idea*] in reference to which all human beings[15] choose and give preference. The fact that thinking and seeing [*phronein kai horan*] are mentioned here, on the one hand, and certain delights [*hēdonai tines*] [1096b17] on the other, correlates nicely with the *Philebus*, where, it will be recalled, certain delights are explicitly allowed. But our passage also speaks of "honors." This addition accords with the ancient doctrine of the three ideals of life, and from Aristotle's point of view, honors should automatically be joined with the other two wherever the concern is politics.) Thus in the *Magna Moralia*

15. Gadamer changed *Seienden* in the text here to *Menschen*. TRANSLATOR.

too, there is no altering the fact that the question about the good is deliberately restricted.

And in similar fashion, the elucidation of the other, inductively derived, concept of the good stays within these confines. For it is the different aretai that are discovered [by induction] to be good.

Thus, this first part of the overall argument does not point beyond itself in the direction of the question on which we have focused our inquiry, that is, the relationship between to agathon (the good) and *to on* (being). Nevertheless, that the question has been narrowed to the specific issue of "the good for us" is noted explicitly in the summary of the *Magna Moralia* at 1183a7, and even more explicitly at the climax of that summary: *"hyper tou agathou ara, kai hyper tou aristou kai hyper tou hēmin aristou"* (about the good and about the best and about the best for us) (1183a23). In this way we are kept aware of the universal, general reference of "the good."

We are made even more clearly aware of this universal reference in the discussion of the concept of the *idea* and what this concept entails. For the postulation of a good in itself plainly derives from Plato's having founded his thinking generally on the ideas: for Plato, "what a thing is most" means in each case "it itself" (*malista* [most] . . . *auto* [itself]). We find this line of thought applied here to the good and, as we mentioned at the beginning, Aristotle even grants that Plato's argument has a certain validity which only in political matters is unimportant and irrelevant. The restricted form that the rejection of Plato's argument takes here becomes even more conspicuous when it comes time to take aim at the more general problems that arise in connection with the universal doctrine of ideas. When it is said then that, in the realm of politics, we are concerned with a class of goods for which the idea of the good has no real relevance as an archē, the idea of the good as such is not called into question—any more than the doctrine of the immortality of the soul, for instance, is called into question when one says that this doctrine has no place in mathematics.[16]

That the overall concern here is with a particular instance of a more general set of problems is made fully clear by the far more universal overtones of Aristotle's way of putting things. When expressions are used here such as *dia tēn hautou physin haireton* (to be chosen according to the nature of it) (1182b9)—which refers back to *en hekastōi tōn ontōn* (in each of the existent things) (1182b8)—this could easily be taken in a universal teleological sense such as is implied, for instance, in the *Eudemian Ethics* at 1218a30, where the reference to Euduxus's doctrine is obvious. In the *Magna Moralia*, to be sure, such general considerations are not pursued per se, even though Aristotle's formulations virtually invite us to pursue them, and even though in his critique of the ideas we find such a universal concept as *ta noēta* (the noetic), which certainly does not make us think primarily of the practical. Quite the contrary: the allusion of ta noēta to the numbers is patent (1183a24), an allusion that, nonetheless, is not stated outright. Instead, the text speaks only of the "idea." This fact notwithstanding, we are dealing here with the same methodological argument that we find in the *Eudemian Ethics* at 1218a16, where it is expressly pointed out that numbers are not generally accepted to be the good. The correspondence to the *Eudemian Ethics* thus shows that the *Magna Moralia* too implicitly points beyond the problems of practical philosophy.

---

16. Dirlmeier makes a convincing case for the *dio* (therefore) at 1183b7. For what follows, the simplest emendation, it seems to me, is: *ouk oikeian archēn einai toutōn tagathon* (the good is not a proper principle of these).

The ontological aspect of the problem of the good is all the more evident in the *Nicomachean Ethics*. Of course, here too the main argument, in which everything culminates, is that the idea of the good is of no practical use (*EN* 1096b33 ff.). But again, even the refutation implies acknowledgment of the issue. Aristotle says explicitly "*ei gar kai estin hen ti to koinēi katēgoroumenon agathon ē chōriston auto kathauto*" (if indeed what is said to be the good in common is one thing or separate and for itself). All the logical arguments against the one common good *kata mian idean* (corresponding to one idea) (1096b25)—the category argument as well as the argument more concerned with pursuing Plato's differentiations of the *kath' hauto haireton* (that which is to be chosen for its own sake) (1098b90)—prove, as it were, uncomfortably more than they should. For it cannot be the case either that "good" is a pure equivocation, that is, that there is one word for completely different things merely coincidentally. Thus Aristotle undercuts his own postion, so to speak. Even though he banishes any consideration of the common element in the use of the word "good" from ethics, he indicates two possible answers to the question of what that common element might be. The first is that the common meaning of "good" being asked about could be thought of as "derived from one thing," that is to say, in such a way that everything (good) "contributes to" (*syntelein*) one thing. Although there is some disparity in the expressions used, there can be no doubt that Aristotle is alluding here to the logical structure that he explicates initially in the *Metaphysics* Gamma 2 and which was later termed the "analogy of attribution." The multiple senses of good do not mean only that the means are good if the end or purpose is good, as the expression *syntelein* might suggest. *Syntelein* must obviously be taken in a wider sense to mean "contributing to a common semantic field," so to speak. The *pros hen* (to one thing) here thus fully accords with the *aph' henos* (from one thing). Accordingly, in the *Metaphysics*, Gamma 2, we find pros hen or *pros mian archēn* (to one principle), respectively,[17] and the example of "healthy," which can be said of a human being, a facial color, a medicine, and so forth. The word "good" could be multivocal in this way too. That would presuppose something privileged and primary such as Aristotle's category doctrine specifies [for "to be"] when it gives priority to "substance" (*ousia*). The priority assigned to "substance" is of great significance for Aristotle's metaphysics, particularly in regard to the theology of the first mover, which, for its part, is first in the order of substances. Given this fact, one might expect that here in the *Nicomachean Ethics* Aristotle would favor such an attributive relationship (*analogia attributiva*) when he sets about grasping the manifold of agathon. The god or nous (intellect), both of which appear as examples of substance in the category argument (*EN* 1096a24), would then be the *summum bonum*, the highest good, in which the attribution terminates. The universal-ontological sense of the one good would fit perfectly with Aristotle's doctrine of a god. The 'theological' conclusion of the *Eudemian Ethics* would also lead us to expect the same thing.[18]

Hence it is all the more surprising that the text continues: "or rather more according to analogy" (*ē mallon kat' analogian*) (1096b28) and makes clear by an example that the bare sameness of the relationships, that is, a proportional analogy, is meant, in which no one thing is given priority over another, and in which there is consequently no terminus.

This concept of proportional analogy, too, is known to us

17. At the same time, the pros hen is characterized as a special case of the more general *kath' hen legesthai* (to speak in one regard).

18. To be sure, *MM* 1182b9 characterizes the question about the good of the god as an *allotria skepsis* (another consideration).

from Aristotle's metaphysics and in other connections as well. In distinction from the later tradition, above all Scholasticism—a tradition that is summed up in Cajetan's famous treatise *De nominum analogia* (*On the Analogy of Names*)—we find in Aristotle simply "analogy." It is self-evident that Aristotle would not consider this universal question more closely in our passage. The whole issue of the common sense of "good" belongs, after all, in the *Metaphysics* and not at all in practical philosophy. This makes it all the more surprising that, nevertheless, here in the *Nicomachean Ethics*, the bare similarity of relationship [or proportional analogy] is the preferred topic. Would one not have thought it much more likely that Aristotle would give preference to the other possibility, the attributive relationship, in order to do justice to the vague question of a highest good, the aristōn pantōn that appeared to be the focus in the *Eudemian Ethics* at 1218b26?[19]

19. As opposed to Aristotle, the later Scholastic tradition which Cajetan recapitulates distinguishes attributive from proportional analogy—to which alone Aristotle refers when he speaks of "analogy." The proportional analogy, or analogy of relationship, is to be found in Aristotle in *Metaphysics* Lambda 4. The point of his argument here is that things that exist do not share any common substance or idea but, rather, only an analogous structure, namely, that of movement from *sterēsis* to eidos (privation to form) or dynamis to energeia (potentiality to actuality), and that each carries out this movement in a way peculiar to it and different from the others. (Cf. Gadamer's translation of, and commentary on, Aristotle's *Metaphysik, Lambda* [Frankfurt, 1948].) Or, put another way, as the eye is actualized in seeing, so, analogously, the ear is actualized in hearing, but *allo allou*, "the one in one way, the other in another." This argument, then, is in critical response to Plato's hypostasis of the ideas: when we say that the soldier who is brave is good or the flautist who is actually playing the flute is good (*EN* 1097b25), there is no single "the good" in itself to be hypostasized here, rather a parallel structure insofar as each, only analogously to the other, does what is appropriate to him. The issue in practical philosophy thus becomes the proper function (*ergon*) or activity (*energeia*) in which human beings find their fulfillment, and any idea of the "good in itself," should it exist at all, is irrelevant here.

To that extent, this Aristotelian line of thought implies an exclusion from prac-

Of course, we see elsewhere that Aristotle is often not entirely decisive, and that in general the carefulness in description and

---

tical philosophy of any theoretical-metaphysical considerations of the one good of all things. Still, Aristotle, precisely by setting such considerations of the one good apart from practical philosophy, confirms that they remain important to him. As Gadamer will point out, Aristotle, like Plato, wants to understand the universe, and not only human practice, as purposive, as aiming at what is best. Therefore, he follows the Platonic Socrates in passing beyond merely material-efficient causal accounts of things.

And it is here that what was later to be called the attributive analogy comes into play: we say that a thing *is* white or *is* larger than something else, and so forth, but before we can say any of these things we must be able to say *what it is*. When we do that, we are not merely articulating a structural parallel, but rather a structural convergence on one ultimate sense of "is," namely, ousia, the "what" or substance, which is the end point in which all the categorially differentiated senses of "is" terminate, and the archē on which they all depend. Aristotle never expressly carries this argument over to our saying "is good," and for the most part he argues, as we have seen, that when we say a flautist is good or a soldier is good, we are speaking of a proportional analogy, an analogy of relationship. But if, for instance, we speak of a healthy food, a healthy facial color, or a healthy person, these different senses and uses are in fact not mere parallels. Rather, as "is" converges on one sense of being, ousia, they converge on one privileged sense of healthy: the terminus, or end point, from which they all derive their meaning is ultimately the health of the human being. Hence the question is: Is there in Aristotle a good in which our diverse uses of the word converge? Can the uses of "good" be said to have a terminus? Lambda 10 makes clear that they can. The best of and for all things, to ariston pantōn, is the good in which the actualization of the individual goods culminates.

The real difference from Plato here results from Aristotle's conception of predication: if we say "is good," we must say that some thing is good, however incorporeal this thing might be—in this instance, the god (*ho theos*). "Good," even the highest good, does not exist independently of the subject that is said to be good. Even good in the highest sense is thus an enhylon eidos. In Plato, on the other hand, the good is an idea that is to be thought of in abstraction from any specific thing and to be analyzed in regard to which other ideas it may be combined with—just as point, line, figure, and solid, are to be considered in their purely mathematical relationships to each other, apart from, say, pointed, curved, square, or cylindrical things. Compare "Amicus Plato Magis Amica Veritas." TRANSLATOR.

analysis that governs him often hinders him from dedicating himself to his own constructive aims, let alone those of his interpreters. As I reminded the reader above, that even holds for Aristotle's metaphysics and still more for the relationships between theoretical and practical philosophy and, within practical philosophy, the relationship between the ideals of political and theoretical life, or even the relationship between political science and political cleverness (*deinotēs*). (We shall return later to this last point.) Sometimes it seems as if Aristotle prefers the analogy structure because it accords particularly well with his descriptive caution. He is inclined to think analogically even in theoretical contexts. Evidently his analogical way of thinking helps him avoid the hypostasis of the universal, or "what is in common." Thus *allo allou* (the one thing in one way, the other in another) is virtually an anti-Platonic catchword *insofar as it underscores the *merely* analogical sameness of things which remain distinct*. Consider, for instance, *Metaphysics*, Lambda, in which Aristotle treats the purely analogical character of the "causes" in lengthy expositions (chapters 3 and 4) and sharply demarcates the entire analysis from any constructive derivation from some single primary reality, and in which, as a consequence, it seems somewhat surprising that at the end the priority of the first mover nevertheless results. When, in the *Nicomachean Ethics*, the pure analogical likeness is given explicit preference, it also sounds as if Aristotle finds that likeness sufficient for the task of conceptualizing the whole teleological order of the world—the program of the *Phaedo*, which in a certain way is his own. In Plato the three great realms of order—soul, state, and world—are similarly represented as analogous, and the good appears in them as that which unifies, gives unity, that is, as the unit, or one.

There is no doubt that in this regard Aristotle shared Plato's view of the world. Even if his own science of the whole is constructed on the very different basis of his physics, and not a mathematical-harmonic conception of the good such as Plato's, he still cannot ignore the Platonic problem as such. That he cannot is audible in our passage in the *Nicomachean Ethics*. How is the good, as that which is in common, to be thought of? Perhaps like being, he says, which we encounter in manifold categoreal differentiation, and which, as we know, is nonetheless the object of a highest science. As a matter of fact, it is in the context of Aristotle's *prima philosophia* that the "pure analogy" first comes into play. We have already mentioned the *Metaphysics*, Lambda 3–4, and Eta 4 also belongs here: although there is no mistaking the anti-Platonic turn it takes, it nonetheless remains an answer to the Platonic problem of the good and being. It is remarkable how much the Platonic problem of the universal dialectic in being—particularly as that dialectic occurs in the *Sophist* and *Parmenides*—evidences itself in many parts of Aristotle's *Metaphysics*, for instance, in the aporiai of Beta and in Gamma. When one compares the way in which the question about being is put there with the context in which the agathon comes up in Plato's *Republic*, *Philebus*, and, indirectly, in his *Timaeus* too, one is struck by the identity of the problem, and the idea of analogy profers itself. What Aristotle rejects as such in Plato's philosophy is not the structural order of the whole but the derivation of that structural order from the hen (one) and the ontological primacy that Plato gives to mathematics as a consequence.

Aristotle saw Speusippus as the prime example of this mathematicizing that a world construed as [proportional] analogies would represent. But of course Plato's doctrine of number and unit is behind Speusippus's theory. After all, there is not only Aristotle's account in the *Metaphysics*, Alpha 6, of the two principles, the one and the indeterminate two, from which all numbers just as all existents in general are derived. The same thing is stated in the *Philebus*'s doctrine of the peras and apeiron, and our linking of Aristotle's account with the *Philebus* is supported by the testimony of Porphyrius cited above, according to which Plato's lecture on the good—of which Porphyrius evidently had Aristotle's original version—can only be made comprehensible by starting with the *Philebus*. The critical point for Aristotle is that the number structure is said to be the structure of being. Here he finds that Plato remained all too Pythagorean.

That is not to say, however, that Aristotle did not have to raise the *metaphysical* question about the good and the best himself. On the contrary, this question is always implied in his question about being. At the end of the grand overview of the whole universe that Book Lambda provides, he formulates an alternative regarding how the nature of the whole might contain the good and the best—either in the form of a best being or in the order of the whole. Here he cannot evade the consequence of the ontological primacy he gives to physics and to physei onta (what is by nature). Plainly, Aristotle is concerned with the unified order of motion in the universe, an order that he defends in opposition to mathematical-harmonic theories in Speusippus's Pythagorean style. Put another way, he is concerned to give physics priority over mathematics—a concern that underlies his well-known objection to the academy, namely, that there philosophy had been turned completely into mathematics. Hence he alludes polemically to Speusippus's Pythagoreanism in the *Nicomachean Ethics*, and in the *Metaphysics*, Lambda 10, in an obviously polemical reference to Speusippus, he rejects a pure [proportional] analogical structure of the universe, citing Homer's well-known "Let the ruler be one" (1076a4).

With that he decides against a mere order and in favor of a good existing apart for itself (*kechōrismenon ti agathon* [a separated good])—although he certainly does not question that each individual order is good. In his eyes, however, the primary reality that he postulates, that which is first (*to prōton*), cannot be something mathematical; rather, it must be a mover, *hōs to kinoun poiei* (such as induces movement). When everything is ordered toward this primary reality, that is indeed "the best of all" (*to ariston pantōn*), and this highest being is at the same time the fulfillment of what being means. Thus, Aristotle puts the Platonic heritage, which the question about the good represents, on the ground of physics. And starting there, he develops his doctrine of being in the conceptual form of an attributive analogy which has a highest *terminus* (end point). 'Pure,' proportional analogy cannot accomplish this—it would remain too close to Platonic ideal mathematics. Hence, we are left with a paradoxical result: the chōrismos (separation) that lives on in Aristotle's theology is not Plato's. On the contrary, the ontology of the physei onta and the entirety of motion as a whole force Aristotle to a chōrismos of his own, which passes beyond Plato's mathematically oriented interpretation of the transcendence of the good.

VI

THE IDEA OF
PRACTICAL PHILOSOPHY

The question now becomes all the more pressing why here, in the *Nicomachean Ethics*, Alpha 4, Aristotle gives preference to the mere analogical structure in inquiry about the good. The reason—which suggests itself at once—could be that he finds the consequence unwelcome that would be implied in *pros hen legesthai* (saying, to one [end]) and in the complete parallel that it establishes. In the *Metaphysics*, Book Gamma, namely, such an attributive proportionality justifies the authority of one and the same science for the entire semantic field of "to be." The examplary case is medicine: "*kathaper kai tōn hygieinōn hapantōn mia epistēmē estin*" (if indeed there is also one science for all matters of health) (1003b11). Where all things converge on one goal [for example, health], a single science is always conceivable. Hence one must obviously interpret the program of a formal ontology elaborated in Book Gamma according to this schema—even if the connection with the books on substance and the theology in Lambda remain obscure by so doing. In any case in regard to the primary science of "being as such" (*on hēi on*), which Aristotle is pursuing, the attributive analogy argument makes good sense. But it would be absurd to claim that it is relevant to the practical question about the good. For that would mean that recognizing a good time for surgery or assessing a good sign in the evening sky promising good weather would be matters for one and the same science, when, in fact, one is a matter for medical science and the other for meterological science. Hence Aristotle has good reason to give preference to the pure proportional analogy.

A science of the "good in general" corresponding to the schema of medicine—a schema that *is* applicable in the science of being in general—is meaningless for practical philosophy. Drawing a parallel with the knowledge of being as such does not work as long as the concern is solely with the structure of human practice and of practical knowledge. Whether it be in regard to technical knowledge or to political-practical knowledge, the good remains restricted [in its application] to the circumstances of human practice. Practical reason is far removed from any universal teleology. Aristotle isolates practical philosophy for the decisive reason that what we find to be good in the theoretical realm—"good" here meaning immutable being—is something quite different from the right thing to do (*to deon*) at which the practical rationality of human beings aims.

This fundamental distinction that Aristotle makes between theoretical and practical knowledge also has consequences for the field of philosophical inquiry that we would call the theory of scientific knowing. At issue is the methodological character of Aristotle's practical philosophy. It is indisputable that practical philosophy itself is not knowledge of the right thing to do in a given situation—this, even though the very fact that the teacher of theoretical instruction in practical philosophy keeps his distance from the more universal questions of ontology, may betray that he does have a knowledge of the right thing to do after all. Be that as it may, practical philosophy has the character of theory. It can be called "*epistēmē*," "*technē*," "*methodos*" (method), "*pragmateia*" (pragmatics), or even "*theōria*" (theory), but not "*phronēsis*" in a terminological sense. Nevertheless, the question arises whether practical philosophy is teachable in the same sense that every other science or technē may be said to be. The state of affairs here becomes even more complicated when we observe that Aristotle disputes that Plato's idea of the good has any practical utility but emphatically asserts that his own theory of practical philosophy does. He claims explicitly that such theoretical instruction as his enhances aretē itself. That it does so is emphasized in all three versions of his ethics. And for just this reason one can see a problem in how practical philosophy is supposed to relate to phronēsis.

This problem has been investigated often in recent times. Still, it probably appears to be a paradox only to someone who has a modernistic understanding of "theoretical," such as we derive from the modern conception of science. For such a person things do indeed appear odd. Plainly, practical philosophy is not a theoretical science in the modern sense — a theoretical science, that is, which might be applied to practice in the way one puts pure natural science to use in [applied] medical science. Practical philosophy is rather more like knowledge of cures, and accordingly, Aristotle often draws comparisons with this kind of knowledge. Any talk of the "application" of theory to practice would presuppose a separation between the theory Aristotle imparts in such an ethical pragmatics [as his ethics] and lived practice. And whatever the case, such a separation does not exist here. The ideal of an objective theory, neutral in regard to all the interests at stake in any practical application of it, and consequently capable of any application one might wish to make, is neither Platonic nor Aristotelian. Our investigation of Plato's science program in the *Republic*, book 7, made clear how secondary the application of the mathematical sciences is in his eyes. Aristotle makes the same point by going to the opposite extreme: in the field of practical philosophy he expressly avoids importing purely theoretical considerations. This restriction holds for his politics and especially for the vast collection of state constitutions that he organized. It is quite clear to him that there is a practical-political problem in just how these model constitutions are to be put to reasonable use—as there is in any application of theoretical general knowledge. (This problem is presented in detail in *EN*, Kappa 10, but it is also implied in *EN*, Zeta 8.)

The system of norms that Aristotle's ethics establishes makes plain that Greek thinking about the polis is tied to empirical contingencies. But this fact does not constitute a theoretical deficiency—any more than the fact that Aristotle advances only those normative insights against contingencies that are sustained by everyone's unquestioned assent. It is characteristic of him that he simply accepts slavery as a natural institution. Plato's normative construct, his ideal city, thus comes much closer to the modern concept of theory, and, as we know, in his utopia Plato explicitly rejects slavery. We have here a methodological contrast expressed repeatedly in Aristotle's critique. In practical philosophy the concern is not with the idea of the good or with the polis that displays consummate justice—even if in his politics Aristotle is not averse to using the ideal model state as a tool in his thinking. Above all else, his concern is with the right thing to do. Thus the true archē (starting point), as he says with startling radicality, is the "that," *to hoti* (*EN* 1095b6, 1098b2). He means that we must start with our practice itself and the living awareness that we have in it of what is *homologoumenon* (agreed upon) as good. With this idea in mind, Aristotle points out that he himself only uses arguments and principles that pertain to the subject matter and then turns this fact critically against Plato (*EE* 1217a10 and, similarly, *MM* 1183b1). In Aristotle's view, if one wants to do practical philosophy, any argument that starts with the good taken as a concept of mathematical harmony is foreign to the subject matter. When he himself makes theoretical assertions about what is good practically—as he indisputably does in his pragmatics—these assertions, he says, are not to be taken from somewhere else but are to be derived from the realm of practical experience itself. For they will then be based on a principle proper to the subject matter (*oikeia archē*).

The statements that Aristotle himself makes in his practical philosophy are, of course, general. And to this extent they all have a theoretical character. They are also not meant at all to be applied to the concrete case of doing the right thing in the way that technical rules are applied in the procedure of producing something. The right thing to do—which one decides on the basis of reasonable, practical deliberation—is not simply a case or instance of a rule. For example, the general structure of aretē that Aristotle elaborates—namely, to be the mean between two extremes—is not a rule that can be applied. The point of his doctrine is not that one has to hold to the golden mean, but that one ought to be aware of what one is actually doing when one does what is right. Extremes are always recognizable here, and a clear consensus exists that they should be rejected whereas what is right as we know, cannot be definitively specified as such.

Nevertheless, Aristotle insists that the theoretical doctrine that he presents as practical philosophy has to be of use in practice. He shows how with an illustration (*EN* 1094a23): practical philosophy, he says, is useful in the way it is useful for an archer to pick out a definite point on the target at which to take aim. This way he will score a better hit. This can only mean that one is better able to keep one's aim fixed in the right direction when one can set one's sights on a specially targeted point instead of on a larger object.[1] Aristotle avails himself of this splendid image to say that the theoretical instruction that can be given in practical philosophy puts in one's hands no rules that one could follow in order to "hit" what is right in accordance with an art (*technē*). After all, taking aim does not by any means constitute the whole of archery. One has to have learned how to handle the bow, and in the same way, whoever wishes to profit from practical philosophy must be trained for it in the right way. Only then is practical philosophy of use in decision making. It assists our concrete, practical ability to size things up insofar as it makes it easier to recognize in what direction we must look and to what things we must pay attention. Plainly the illustration is intended to show that one does not rely on the theoretical generalities of practical philosophy in the way that one relies on a rule.[2]

To be sure, Aristotle models his exposition of the exercise of

1. In Plato we encounter the word *skopos* as the expression for that at which one aims (*stochazesthai*) at *Republic* 519c, *Gorgias* 507d, and elsewhere, and often in Aristotle, but never with direct reference to archery. Nevertheless, this semantic origin is implied at least once, namely at *EN*, Zeta 1, 1138b22, where tightening and loosening (*epitenei kai aniesin*) must surely be taken in reference to the bow and not the lyre. In all other respects the semantic field of these two words is coextensive. Cf. Heraclitus, fragment 51.

2. The point here is relevant to the contemporary Anglo-American debate concerning rules in rule deontologism (for example, D. Ross), in rule utilitarianism (for example, R. Brandt), and contractualism (for example, J. Rawls). Cf. in particular the latter's "Two Concepts of Rules," *Philosophical Review* 64 (1955):3–32). The question that Gadamer raises, starting from Aristotle, is an ontological-epistemological one: What is the existential status of moral rules, and how can we be said to "know" them when we apply them? He is at pains to show that the methodological models of the mathematical sciences and technology are misplaced here. For the "being" of the rule or ethical principle is not like that of "triangularity," that is, not like the being of something that is always apart from its instantiations and toward which the latter may be said to "strive" while nevertheless always falling short. On the contrary, rules in ethics have their reality only in the tradition of their applications, instantiations, or interpretations. And each of these, far from being a diminution of some ideal rule in itself

practical reason entirely on the logic of the theoretical syllogism used in demostration (*apodeixis*). But some precise distinctions are necessary here. Certainly every reasonable conclusion to which one comes can be depicted using the schema of a syllogism. It is also easy to see that in the sphere of practice the conclusion (*Schluss*) is not a proposition but a decision (*Entschluss*). Still, it is striking that when Aristotle analyzes the exercise of this practical reason, he does not use decisions that are really practical or moral, but pragmatic, technical decisions instead. In the technical realm the only concern is with the right choice of means for pre-given ends or purposes. At the heart of the matter here is the subsumption of the particular under the universal, and the structural correspondence with *apodeixis* is thereby given. But one should not overlook the fact that making moral decisions does not quite fit this schema. For in the realm of practice, holding to a principle, for example, to a certain aretē, is not a merely logical act. Practical reasonableness is displayed not only in knowing how to find the right means but also in holding to the right ends.

Aristotle's demarcation of *phronimos* (prudent, reasonable)

---

apart from its instantiations, is thus to be viewed as an "accretion of reality" (Gadamer: *Zuwachs an Sein*) in the rule.

This understanding of the reality of ethical rules requires that we revise our conception of how we know them. We do not know them as we know mathematical realities, that is "clearly and distinctly," as objects to be intuited purely and exactly in abstraction from situational contingencies. Rather, we know them only in a limited way from within the tradition of their applications, in which we always already find ourselves "under way" (*unterwegs*). Consequently, the same measure of exactitude is not to be expected here as in the mathematical sciences and technology (Cf. *EN* 1094b24). Indeed, this kind of rigor would be disastrous: *summum ius summa injuria*. Phronēsis, understanding of moral principles, is thus anything but being a "stickler" for the rules. It is judicious discretion that, in faithfulness to the tradition, adjusts to the particularities of the given case (Cf. Gadamer on Aristotle's *dikastē phronēsis* and *synesis* in *WM*). TRANSLATOR.

from *deinos* (clever) turns on this point (*EN*, Zeta 13). In this distinction one sees how very much aware Aristotle is of the difference between technical knowing and practical-moral knowing, and I have attempted to show that here he extends a genuinely Platonic motif. Not the least indication that he does so is the fact that no real teaching is possible here in the way in which science and technical knowledge can be taught. On the contrary, in practical matters the general hermeneutical task which figures in all instances, that is, of concretizing general knowledge, always implies the opposite task of generalizing something concrete.

Practical philosophy by itself can give us no assurance that we know how to "hit" what is right. Such knowledge remains the end of practice itself and the virtue of a practical reasonableness (*phronēsis*), which is precisely not mere inventiveness (*deinotēs*). This distinction is important for the theory of the sciences. The comparison with the archer is found in the introduction to Aristotle's whole course on practical philosophy and politics. At the start, the governing role played by politics is worked out. Politics is the highest science or art: "*kuriōtatē kai malista architektonikē*" (first of the arts, worthiest and greatest) (*EN* 1094a26).

At first glance this comment bearing on the theory of scientific knowing would not seem to accord all that well with the subsequent analysis of phronēsis and especially not with what is said about political phronēsis. Ever since Burnet, this discrepancy has been attributed to Aristotle's having accommodated himself to Plato's use of language. Viewed purely on the surface of it, this account is certainly accurate. But Aristotle could not possibly have spoken in any other way. For we saw, after all, that in practical philosophy we are dealing precisely with philosophy, which is to say with theory. Its object and, accordingly, what it ultimately is aimed at, is, of course, practice. But that only means that its method must be subordinated to the law governing its object, which entails in turn that its claim to know is defined and restricted in accordance with that law. What Aristotle calls "*ēthos*" (habituation) is of fundamental importance for human practice. Whoever cannot master his passions is not in a position to listen to the logos (reason).[3] Aristotle particularly impresses this fact on us one last time at the very end of his lecture. And the fact that he does, shows us that he was fully aware of the impli-

---

3. *Auf den logos zu hören*. There is a long tradition behind this phrase, extending to Heidegger's—and then Gadamer's—interpretation of Heraclitus (Cf. Heidegger, *Heraklit*, part 2, "Logik. Heraklits Lehre vom Logos" [Frankfurt, 1979]). Heidegger finds in Heraclitus an explication of the inauthentic existence of those who are caught in the patterns of their everyday pursuits, and who, unthinking and deaf, remain oblivious to the logos, the reasonable order in the many evanescent things with which they are absorbed (Heraclitus: *ta panta*). Note that the word *hören* is of particular significance here: the logos is not something I see before me and over which I may be said to dispose. It is rather more like significant sound, or language, by which I am surrounded and within which I "always already" find myself under way.

Heidegger's concern, of course, is not so much praxis but theōria, even if the latter is to be understood not so much as visual but as aural. Here Gadamer makes the transition to the practical, as he did beginning with his first book, *PDE*. But as this chapter of the present book confirms, he discovers a continuity between logos in practice and logos in theōria: any individual caught in the unrestrained play of the passions and the immediate, unreflective pursuit of gratification is incapable of the highest human activity, a life of reason—incapable, that is, of a life of reason in its practical dimension, but also, and importantly, in its theoretical dimension as well. Sophrosynē, for instance, is a prerequisite of sophia. And reciprocally, in some sense sophia, or at least philosophia, which liberates the human being from the "flattery" and coercion of the passions, is a prerequisite for sophrosynē. Plato and Aristotle both teach us that.

Thus one sees in Gadamer's reading of Plato and Aristotle just how one might extend Heidegger's thinking about being, and his theory of our obliviousness to being to include practical philosophy. This extension would lead to an ethics of aretē and not at all the ethics of *agapē* for which, apparently, Werner Marx claims to have found a basis in Heidegger (Cf. W. Marx, *Gibt es auf Erden ein Mass* [Hamburg, 1983]). TRANSLATOR.

cations of the structure of practice for the theory of scientific knowing. Clearly a special prerequisite for receiving instruction in practical philosophy is that the pupil will not fall victim to the misunderstanding to which technical thinking gives rise— namely, that such instruction could relieve him of his own practical responsibility. To be sure, that is never stated explicitly. However, this consequence for the theory of scientific knowing, which is intrinsic to the idea of practical philosophy, is made evident indirectly at the end of the lecture, when Aristotle prepares for the transition to politics. There he explicitly repudiates political theoreticians who, as sophists, claim authority in the matter of giving constitutions and laws without actually being in political life themselves. The claim Aristotle makes for his own political philosophy and his insistence that the pupil have the right preparation ahead of time are in response to this sophistic claim.

A separate investigation would be necessary to establish more precisely the locus of Aristotle's politics within the theory of scientific knowing. In the treatise called the *Politics* we find no special methodological reflection, evidently because the beginning of the *Nicomachean Ethics* is conceived of as the general methodological introduction to the whole of politics. The conclusion of the *Nicomachean Ethics*, which makes the transition to politics, takes up this theme again explicitly. Of course, the version of the *Politics* that we have is not very well connected to this transition. Hence one might well question the extent to which this treatise on the polis is subject to particular requirements of its own field of inquiry—requirements that are not the general ones of practical philosophy as such. For it is clear that the concern in this political treatise is lawgiving. The art of lawgiving, however, is certainly very different from anything in political or juridical decision making, both of which are confronted with concrete cases. In the *Nicomachean Ethics* 1141b the art of lawgiving is explicitly distinguished from the other applications of political reason. One methodological observation which could result from this distinction might be, for example, that one ought not to change existent laws in favor of better ones without including in one's calculation the fact that any change in the laws is bad to the extent that it necessarily weakens the authority of law in general (*Politics* 1263a12 ff.).

Aristotle's reflections on the method of practical philosophy thus have important consequences for the theory of scientific knowing, but this is not the place to pursue the significance of these for our own situation and its special problems. Aristotle's separation of practical philosophy from theoretical philosophy has demonstrated its power to establish and sustain a tradition—this, not least of all, in recent centuries in which his distinction between the two has been challenged by the idea of modern empirical science. To be sure, his distinction was no longer able to maintain a real place for itself within the methodological reflections of modern science—other than in the weak afterglow of the rhetorical tradition that Vico, for instance, once again invoked. Nevertheless, the fact that the philological, historical sciences have actually spread within the cosmos of modern science proves that this tradition is not dead. The relevance of these so-called human sciences to the moral, political, and social circumstances of human life is convincingly demonstrated if one considers the role played in these by world views, ideologies, and enduring human value concepts. In this regard I would call to mind, for instance, the contribution that the historical sciences have made in determining the identity of modern nation states, and continue to make to the present day. And not least important of all, certainly, is the tradition of practical philosophy itself. It is a fact worth noting that philosophical ethics has almost never renounced its right to inject its normative judgments into life as it is actually lived. To this extent Aristotle lives on. The theoretical and practical processes of reflection in human reason seem in the end to be indissociably intertwined. One can properly understand this correlation of the two only if, following Aristotle, one strives to keep the idea of theoretical constructs and of scientific method out of the practical field, and only if one recognizes that the relationship of theoretical insight to practical application is not as simple everywhere as it is in the fields of technology.[4]

The clearest exposition of this theme, which Aristotle was the first to take up, seems to me to be Kant's *Foundations of a Metaphysics of Morals*. There, at the conclusion of the first section on the so-called "laying of the groundwork," Kant treats the transition from common reasonable moral knowledge to philosophical knowledge. He starts with the convincing thesis that in human nature as such there is a proclivity at work: human beings tend to resort to a kind of dialectic in order to evade what their consciousness of duty, for instance, makes morally evident to them. Kant calls this a tendency to quibble, and it not only makes the transition to the philosophy of morals necessary, but essentially always makes that transition by itself. It is obvious that Kant adheres to the basic tenet of Platonic-Aristotelian phi-

---

4. Aristotle's language usage reflects the [unity of the theoretical and practical] in a way that should not be taken as [just] an echo of Plato, for example, at *EN* 1177a14–15: *"eite dē nous touto eite allo ti, ho dē kata physin dokei archein kai hēgeisthai kai ennonian echein peri kalōn kai theiōn"* (whether this is the intellect or something else which we believe by its nature rules and guides us and envisions things noble and divine). Here it appears completely artificial to attempt to distinguish between the theoretical and practical exercise of reason. And even if in the *Protrepticus* (Walzer, fragment 6) they are distinguished, and practical dianoia and theoretical contemplation of the truth are treated separately, they are nevertheless characterized using the same words, and both are demarcated from all knowledge in *poiēsis* (making something).

losophy in his moral philosophy, insofar as he divorces the practical, moral imperative from the technical imperative of cleverness. But that is not all; his exposition of the transition from common to philosophical knowledge, has, it seems to me, universal validity. Philosophy never really finds it necessary to justify its existence, since whoever would contest it is also engaging in the process of reflection that one calls philosophy.

In returning to Aristotle, we find the intertwining of the theoretical and practical that we have seen at many sorts of cracks and splits in the structure of his teachings. For one thing, we see that according to Aristotle the highest possibility of awareness, which the Greeks called "*nous*" (intellection), is to be attributed to that theoretical knowing which has attained complete self-fulfillment—to sophia (wisdom). But the same highest awareness is to be attributed to practical reason as well—namely, to phronēsis, which in each instance is conscious of the rightness of its choice and decision. The definitive juxtaposition of theoretical and practical knowing, and hence of the theoretical and practical virtues of knowing, in no way infringes upon the unity of reason, which governs us in both these directions [in which our reasoning might move].

Aristotle's conception of a "practical philosophy" is plainly the consequence of the critique we treated above of Plato's idea of the good. Nevertheless, his separation of practical philosophy from theoretical philosophy in no way implies a lack of coherence or an inconsistency in the content [of his thought]. On the contrary, it is solely out of methodological and argumentative caution that Aristotle forbids himself any and every extension [of his practical thought] into more universal considerations. Not that such a universal, more theoretical background does not show through in many places. But Aristotle makes use of it in his argument only where it is based in universally accepted, given facts that provide a methodological foundation for theoretical philosophy too.

Naturally Aristotle does not speak of practical philosophy in the context of his metaphysics. But insofar as the world of human practice is located within the entirety of what exists, the whole sphere of human praxis (action) and poiēsis (doing) has its place within the realm of nature. Not only art imitates nature. Human practice does so too insofar as it aims at nothing other than the highest fulfillment of human existence itself. The fact that it does, however, shows that at the same time human existence points beyond itself [to the divine]. And hence Aristotle too—in following where necessity leads him—must give precedence to the theoretical ideal of life as opposed to practice and politics.

Within his practical philosophy this precedence is also made clear by the ontological implications of Aristotle's concepts— something that cannot be pursued here in detail. Let it suffice to call attention to one point: the paradigm of being that always is—be it the being of the divine or of the heavenly bodies—remains the ultimate point of reference in treating the practical nature of the human being. Thus on occasion it is said that human nature per se is "not simple" (*EN* 1154b21) or that it is "compounded" (*EN* 1177b28); it does not consist in the pure intellectuality of any divine living thing. Nevertheless, nous (intellection, mind), or logos (reason), is the most important component in us, and it is our task to develop it above all the others.

In general, human beings are vulnerable to their drives and feelings (*pathē*), which threaten to overwhelm them. Still, the essence of human practice lies in the fact that we do not simply give ourselves over to the forces of these drives. Instead, we are capable of cultivating in ourselves a constant disposition (*hexis*), so to speak, which enables us to obey our reason, the logos. This

capacity too is human nature. Aristotle explicitly emphasizes
that it is, when he characterizes the realm of praxis and ēthos,
which takes shape in habituation and habit, as specifically human. He thereby distinguishes it from everything that is by nature (*pephykosin hēmin* [has come to be in us by nature]) (*EN*
1103a25).⁵ The teleological framework into which the entire

5. Gadamer has already shown that in regard to habituation and habit,
where many have seen Aristotle departing from Plato's "over-intellectualization"
of practical philosophy, Plato and Aristotle are in fact very much alike. Plato's
entire *Republic* may be viewed as a program of *training*, leading not only, and
not even primarily, to insight into what the good is, but to an inculcated disposition (*hexis*, *ēthos*) to hold to the good in practice (Cf. "Plato's Educational
State").

On this point Gadamer also finds Kant (and Kierkegaard) to be within the
"unitary effect" of Platonic-Aristotelian philosophy. According to Kant, I must
be made immune to the "sophistic" whisperings of my inclinations, for these
might lead me to deviate from what my reason and conscience tell me is obligatory (see *MPE* and ch. 3 n. 12, above). It is possible that Gadamer is able to discern this "holding to one thing" in Socrates, Plato, and Aristotle precisely in retrospect from Kierkegaard (cf. *WM* 91). So one might argue that in Gadamer,
Heidegger's use of Kierkegaard for the purposes of an ontological explication of
the being of the human being is reversed: Heidegger's "*existentiales*" concern
again becomes Kierkegaard's "existentielles" concern.

However, while Kierkegaard and the early Heidegger spoke of the *existentielle*
"decision" of the solitary individual, Gadamer, in returning to the classical
thinkers, speaks of deliberation and choice (*prohairesis*) founded in a communal
sense of what is fitting (*to deon*; *das Tunliche*). "I" am ethical by virtue of participation in the language, customs, and practices (*Sitten*) which "we" are: "Each
single individual who raises himself from his natural being to a life of spirit, finds
in the language, customs and institutions of his people a pre-given substance,
and, as in learning language, it is his task to make it his own. Thus the single individual is always in the process of cancelling his physical aspect insofar as the
world into which he grows is a world shaped by language and custom" (*WM* 11).
(See ch. 2, n. 9, above.)

In general, Gadamer's divergence in ethics from existentialism's solitary individual may be said to parallel Heidegger's "turn" away from the fundamental
ontology of *SZ*. Just as Heidegger abandons any attempt to build a theory of being on the "acts" of the human subject and, on the contrary, defines human exis-

practical world is fitted could be similarly displayed in many passages. Doubtless, for Aristotle too, the structural order that is to be attributed to this whole of things can be conceived of in reference to the good. That it can may be deduced from the fact that Aristotle finds his teleological cause (*aitia*) missing in all his predecessors. The teleological cause, together with the doctrine of the eidos, is Platonic inheritance. Thus Aristotle has no problem at all in calling the teleological cause the cause of the "well" (*eu*) (*Metaphysics* 984b11) or even the *hou heneka kai tagathon* (that for the sake of which and the good) (!) (983a31), and thus in using exactly the same word that Plato uses.

One should not view this choice of words as a remnant of [Aristotle's 'early'] Platonism, and certainly not as a basis for dating texts. Rather, in these cases too, such language usage confirms that the problem Aristotle treats is one both he and Plato see.

The strongest confirmation of what they share, however, is to be found in the way that Aristotle holds fast to the ideal of theoretical life. That, of course, is made clear above all in the arrangement of the *prōto philosophia*, in particular in its so-called theology. But the lecture on practical philosophy also concludes with a corresponding discussion of the relationship between the theoretical and practical ideal of life. The priority of theōria is based on the ontological superiority of its objects, namely, beings that always are. In contrast, the world of praxis belongs to that reality or being that can be one way but also be another. Consequently, knowledge of what is to be done in practice must be placed second to theōria. Even so, both dispositions of know-

---

tence starting with being's "presencing" to the human being, so too, Gadamer defines human choice (*prohairesis*) in starting with tradition, which surpasses any individual. TRANSLATOR.

ing and reason are something supreme. Practical reasonableness, phronēsis, as well as theoretical reasonableness are "best-nesses" (*aretai*).[6] That which is highest in the human being—which Aristotle likes to call "nous" or the divine—is actualized in both of them.[7]

In this paradoxical doctrine which affirms [the] subordination [of one thing to another] and nevertheless acknowledges two forms of one highest thing, we find displayed the same descriptive carefulness in Aristotle's thinking that we discussed in the context of the problem of analogy. The cautious formula of analogical thinking ["the one thing in one way, the other in another"] indeed proves its worth in this final and highest problem of practical philosophy. We can establish the priority of theōria on the basis of practical philosophy alone, without having to bring in the subject matter of theoretical philosophy. Practice itself is the all-inclusive, distinctive characteristic of the human being. Thus, one must understand even theoretical activity as highest praxis (*Politics* 1325b). Aristotle remains quite vague in discussing the relationships here. At the end of his treatment of phronēsis (*EN*, Zeta 13) he argues that the inclusiveness of human practice entails no subordination of theory to practice.

6. W. Schadewald proposed this non-word, which, better than any other expression for *aretē*, brings out the decisive point here.

7. Aristotle often says that everything that *is* in some way or other participates in the divine. Of course, this does not mean that the *alla zōia* (other living things) participate in eudaimonia—apart from the "*kata tēn epōnamian en tēi physei metechei theiou tinos*" (whatever in the realm of nature, which in accord with what it is named after, takes part in something divine) (*EE* 1217a24). This passage must be explained differently from all proposals to date. *Epōnumai* (things named after . . .) is used in a seminal sense and refers to particular animals that are to be assigned to a god and can therefore be called divine, such as a stallion (Homer) or a bird (for example, Zeus's eagle) or a fish. (Is Aristotle thinking here of the sacred dolphin of Apollo?) In explaining the passage *EE* 1217a25 ff., I would go even further than Dirlmeier's telling criticism of Gigon.

Practical reasonableness, though, is the precondition for engaging in theory and in developing theoretical reasonableness. At the same time, practical reasonableness is also something highest. Indeed, it is this same highest thing, nous—albeit in another application which is not reducible to theory but which is also a *beltistē hexis tou alētheuein* (a most excellent disposition of knowing truly).

With that a final and substantive similarity between Plato's philosophy and Aristotle's practical philosophy comes into view. It turns on the relationship [of human life] to the divine, a relationship which both take as the starting point for their thinking on the finite, conditional, and limited nature of the human being. Aristotle can repeat genuinely Platonic ways of putting things when he attempts to describe the approximation of the human being to the divine. What Hegel claims—namely, that philosophy itself must surpass its character of striving for knowledge and become wisdom—may not be said for Aristotle.

On that account one may not absolutize the priority given to the ideal of theoretical life over the ideal of practical-political life; Aristotle knows just as well as Plato that for human beings precisely this possibility of the theoretical life is limited and conditional. Human beings cannot devote themselves persistently and uninterruptedly to thought's pure seeing for precisely the reason that their nature is composite. Hence, viewed from the perspective of practical philosophy, the relationship of the two ideals of life is not such that the complete happiness of practical life would not be something supreme too. To be sure, Aristotle calls this happiness a *deuteros*, that is, a second best. But this too is something best, that is, a fulfillment of eudaimonia (happiness). The fulfillment in purely theoretical existence is, after all, not the full bliss of the gods, since it is a limited fulfillment for

human beings. The happiness of nous is in a certain sense separate (kechōrismenē)—beyond all comparison. And precisely for
this reason the practical happiness of human beings is not second
rank, rather precisely what has been apportioned to them. That
holds even if at times they can also rise beyond themselves to the
divine bliss of theōria. Does one not find the same thing in
Plato's Republic in regard to how the philosopher-kings will
carry out their office?

Thus the overall result of our investigation is as follows: in
basing the question about being on the physei onta and not on
the universality of the eidos or mathematical-eidetic configura-
tions, Aristotle did indeed subject Plato's teachings to a radical
critique. But in the end did he not carry out what Plato intended
to do—indeed, even go beyond it in fulfilling it? There are basic
truths that the Socratic Plato did not lose sight of any more than
did the Platonic Aristotle: in human actions the good we project
as hou heneka (that for the sake of which) is concretized and
defined only by our practical reason—in the euboulia (well-
advised-ness) of phronēsis. Furthermore, every existent thing is
"good" when it fulfills its telos (purpose, goal). Still, Plato only
anticipated symbolically in his number doctrine what the good
in such a universal sense actually means. Aristotle found conceptual answers to this question. The artificial expression entelech-
eia, which Aristotle introduces, is obviously supposed to make
clear precisely that the telos is not a goal that belongs to some
faraway order of perfection. Rather, in each case the telos is realized in the particular existent itself, and realized in such fashion
that the individual contains the telos. Aristotelian metaphysics
keeps this fact in focus as its constant theme. It thinks of the being of what is as the self-mediation of an existent thing with its
"what-it-is" (ti estin), its eidetic determination. I have tried to

make credible that such a mediation of being and becoming[8] has
to be presupposed if the postulation of ideas is to make any sense
at all. The idea of the good and the barely comprehensible doctrine of the one and the two, point to ʒuch a mediation even
though it is formulated only metaphorically in Plato's dialogues—in the game played in the *Parmenides*, the likeness of
the *Philebus*, or the mythos of the *Timaeus*. In Aristotle's
thought, what Plato intended is transferred to the cautious and
tentative language of philosophical concepts.

---

8. *Vermittlung von Sein und Werden*. Such a mediation is, of course, precisely the task that Hegel sets himself in his *Logik*. One should not overlook the
Hegelian background in Gadamer's analysis of Plato and Aristotle (cf. "Hegel
and Dialectic of the Ancient Philosophers". TRANSLATOR.

INDEX

Aisthēsis (perception), 12, 45, 45n13
Aitia (cause), 25, 93–94, 108, 114, 137n, 174
Alexander, 14
Allo allou (the one thing in one way, the other in another, 153n, 155, 175. See also Analogy
Analogy, 29, 66, 124, 131, 155–56, 175; of attribution, 151, 152, 153n, 158; of proportion, 152, 153, 153n, 160
Anamnēsis (recollection), 45–55, 57–59. See also Pre-knowledge of aretē
Anaxagoras, 15; on nous, 25
Apeiron (the indefinite), 91, 108, 112–14, 122, 157
Apology, 23, 34, 39, 110
Archē (first principle), 25, 29, 90, 91, 93, 94, 100, 137n, 150; as to hote (the "that"), 162. See also Prōton
Aretē, 22, 23, 37, 42, 52, 128, 147; versus technē, 23, 32–34, 46, 49; as unteachable, 50, 51, 60 (see also dialectic and phronēsis); unity of in phronēsis, 63–66; and practical philosophy, 161; as hitting the mean, 163
Ariston pantōn (best of all, highest good), 129–30, 129n, 146, 153n, 158
Arithmos. See Number doctrine

The Beautiful, 77, 115–16, 124–25, 133n, 137

Becoming. See Genesis
Being, 5, 98, 117, 131, 138, 139–40, 158–59; coming into, 13, 114; relationship of to the good, 27, 149, 156, 160; that always is, 171, 174; question about, 177–78. See also Substance

Categories, 13n, 15n13, 16
Category argument, 131, 139–42, 151–52. See also Substance
Cave, allegory of, 74, 76–79, 100
Chōrismos (separation), 9–10, 12, 16–20, 31, 113, 131–32, 135, 138–39, 142–43; in moral phenomena, 18–19; in logic, 19; in Aristotle, 133n, 158
Clitopho, 22, 49
Courage (andreia), 64–65, 95, 142
Crito, 97

De Anima on active and passive nous, 89
"Developmental" interpretation of Plato and Aristotle, 7–9, 38, 103, 135n, 138n
Dialectic, 5, 20, 83, 84, 92, 109; as unteachable, 37; as phronēsis not technē, 39, 121; as holding steadfastly to what is right, 41–43, 96–97; as the art of distinguishing where confusion threatens, 44–45, 95, 98–99; versus dianoia, 90–92, 100; in the arts of music and letters, 119–21

179